New York University
CENTER FOR INTERNATIONAL STUDIES
Studies in Peaceful Change

WHY FEDERATIONS FAIL: An Inquiry into the Requisites for Successful Federalism
Thomas M. Franck, Gisbert H. Flanz, Herbert J. Spiro and Frank N. Trager.
New York: New York University Press, 1968

A FREE TRADE ASSOCIATION
Thomas M. Franck and Edward Weisband.
New York: New York University Press, 1968

LAW, REASON AND JUSTICE: Essays in Legal Philosophy
Graham B. Hughes.
New York: New York University Press, Spring 1969

COMPARATIVE CONSTITUTIONAL PROCESS
Thomas M. Franck.
New York: Frederick A. Praeger, Inc.; London: Sweet & Maxwell Ltd., 1968

THE STRUCTURE OF IMPARTIALITY
Thomas M. Franck.
New York: The Macmillan Company, 1968

AGENTS OF CHANGE: A Close Look at the Peace Corps
David Hapgood and Meridan Bennett.
Boston: Little, Brown and Company, 1968

INTERNATIONAL BUSINESS NEGOTIATIONS: A Study in India
Ashok Kapoor.
New York: New York University Press, 1970

SIERRA LEONE: An Experiment in Democracy in an African Nation
Gershon Collier.
New York: New York University Press, 1970

MICROSTATES AND MICRONESIA: Problems of America's Pacific Islands and other Minute Territories
Stanley A. de Smith
New York: New York University Press, 1970

Czechoslovakia
Intervention and Impact

Studies in Peaceful Change

Prepared under the auspices of
The Center for International Studies, New York University.

New York: New York University Press
London: University of London Press Ltd
1970

Czechoslovakia Intervention and Impact

by I. William Zartman

© 1970 by New York University
Library of Congress Catalog Card Number: 72-111523
SBN: 8147-0488-3
Manufactured in the United States of America

Dedicated to
Stanislav Myslil
and the other Czechoslovaks
who inspire us

Preface

The Soviet invasion of Czechoslovakia in August, 1968, troubled the minds of many observers who had hitherto seen subtle signs of a change in intrabloc and East-West relations. The Center for International Studies at New York University took the occasion in early December to subject the events of the preceding months to academic inquiry, by holding a conference on "The Impact of the Czechoslovak Events on Current International Relations." This volume presents the conference materials to a wider audience.

The five papers prepared for the conference by Professor Jan Triska of Stanford University, Professor William Griffith of the Massachusetts Institute of Technology, Professor Andrew Scott of the University of North Carolina, Professor Vernon Aspaturian of the Pennsylvania State University, and Dr. Andrew Pierre of the Hudson Institute and Columbia University have been revised for this collection. Mr. Helmut Sonnenfeldt of the Department of State was the luncheon speaker. As in any such conference, the real value of the meeting lies in the exchange of ideas among the participants, based on their papers and on their own experiences, yet the transcript of the discussions did not lend itself readily to verbatim publication. In an effort to make as much of this exchange as possible available to readers, the discussion has been edited into a concluding chapter by Professor I. William Zartman of New York University, who organized the conference. It is hoped that both the diversity and the direction of the discussion have been preserved.

The Center for International Studies is grateful to all those who made the conference possible, and especially to the participants. These, in addition to the co-authors of this volume, include Professor Donald Blackmer of the Massachusetts Institute of Technology; Professor Robert Bowie of Harvard University; Mr. William Clark of the World Bank; Professors Vera Dean, Gisbert Flanz, Thomas Franck, and Gidon Gottlieb of New York University; Mr. Emile Guikovaty of *l'Express;* Professor John Hazard of Columbia University; Professor W. W. Kulski of Duke University; Professor Eugen Loebl of Vassar College; Professor Gregory Massell of Princeton University; Mr. Roman Michalowski of New York University; Professor A. F. K. Organski of the University of Michigan; Professor Ellsworth Raymond of New York University; Professor Stephen Schwebel of the American Society of International Law; Mr. Harry Schwartz of *The New York Times;* Mr. Helmut Sonnenfeldt of the Department of State; Mr. Alan Stroock of Stroock, Stroock and Lavan; Mr. Paul Wohl of the *Christian Science Monitor;* Mr. Edward Weisband of New York University; Professor Paul Zinner of the University of California, Davis; and Mr. David Hapgood, Professor Robert Hawkins, Professor Kyung-Won Kim, Professor Michael O'Leary, Mr. Henri Reymond, Professor Werner Ruf, and Professor Louis Sohn, Senior Fellows at the Center for International Studies, New York University.

I. William Zartman

Contents

Foreword

The events of August 1968 took Americans by surprise, rather more than have most contemporary international events. Even hardened, professional analysts of international affairs had come to believe that we were in an era of detente, bridge-building and multipolarity. The second volume of this *Studies in Peaceful Change* series contains this statement, characteristic of its time (early 1968) :

> Since total war has given way to political maneuvering as the accepted means to expand the national interest, and since a pragmatic plurality of objectives has replaced the simplistic formulae of unrelenting, universal struggle as the style of international relations, it is natural that the coalitions and blocs formed in an earlier wartime and postwar-period of simple bipolarity should yield to a greater diversity of policy and motive not only between but *within* global alliances.

The Soviet invasion of Czechoslovakia shocks us, not solely on account of its brutality, but also because it so radically departed from the informed expectations of many country-experts and international systems analysts.

This book incorporates an attempt by scholars to begin to deal with the challenging questions which follow an unpredicted event. Did Russia's conduct indicate a sharp shift in

Soviet policies and priorities, or merely a return to long-term means and ends which had been temporarily modified for tactical reasons? Did the policies of the U.S.—what we did, and what we did not do—make the invasion easier and less costly for Moscow? Should Czechoslovakia be considered the model for, or an exception to, future expectations of Soviet conduct? What were the key determinant variables in the Soviet decision? In this volume Professor Zartman and those scholars he assembled for this project contribute significantly to our understanding of these somber events, and so help us towards the formulation of a foreign policy responsive to the new conditions of post-Czechoslovakian international reactions. A second study, in this same series, *The Johnson Doctrine and the Brezhnev Doctrine,* will continue these investigations.

Professor Thomas M. Franck,
    Director
Center for International Studies
New York University
New York, New York

Czechoslovakia
Intervention and Impact

Political Change in Czechoslovakia and the Soviet Intervention

by Jan F. Triska

Different stages of economic development in East European Communist Party states call for different economic organizations; those which fit one developmental stage manifestly do not fit another. The failure of the Stalinist mobilization system —which may have been suitable for an earlier developmental stage of forced industrialization but not for a more complex advanced stage—has created irresistible pressures for changes in the basic patterns of production, distribution, consumption, and control.[1]

Changes in these economic patterns have significant social consequences. The nascent economic organizations tend to produce social structures different from those produced by preceding economic organizations. The new social structures, once established, tend to press for corresponding changes in the structure of authority. In other words, the more functional requisites change, the greater the push for change in political decision-making.

In Eastern Europe, in addition, the ruling party elites perceive economic organization as the independent variable which conditions and determines the socio-political structure. The functional requisites of the advanced industrialized polity

1

thus not only do call for appropriate translation into the output structures, into political authority—they are expected to do so. Party elites in Eastern Europe are thus not only bound to respond politically to the increasing economic complexity of their respective systems, but, given their own basic mission as modernizers and socializers, they know they must do so.

Unfortunately, the East Europeans are not masters in their own houses, for their structural domestic changes have foreign policy implications. The intervening variable here is the perception and evaluation of the changes by the Soviet elite as to the effect on their own interests. The Soviet intervention in Czechoslovakia in August, 1968, illustrates the point.

ECONOMIC CHANGES

Let me explain and amplify these four related propositions, starting with the first statement, namely, that different stages of economic development in a political system call for different economic organizations.

The Stalinist economic mobilization system, with its sustained emphasis on forced development of heavy industry to the neglect of almost everything else, may be perceived as a suitable economic structure for backward nations eager to catch up with the modern world. But, as the spectacular failure of the Czechoslovak economy proved in the early sixties, the Stalinist economic organization is not suited to more advanced stages of economic development.

The New Economic Model, hesitantly endorsed by the desperate Party leadership of Czechoslovakia in 1967, professed the need to free the economy from exaggerated centralization, administrative rigidity, and the inflexibility of articifial price-fixing. The New Model stipulated that market prices should reflect realistic trade prices for services and commodities in order to eliminate the discrepancy between supply and demand. For this reason, the character and role

of money had to be changed, the new economic blueprint pos-
tulated, to become the most important yardstick for assessing
the "social necessity" of particular work forms, that is,
purchasable work. But the principal target was the human
motivation under socialism—the professed need to motivate
people to work more and better. An advanced economy does,
indeed, depend upon motivating individuals to purchase a
higher standard of living through stratified higher real wages,
the reformers argued.[2]

However, the New Economic Model put into force on
January 1, 1967, was a half-hearted compromise, which little
resembled the original far-reaching reform proposed by the
economic planners. The Party elite, despite its mildly positive
attitude toward the Model and its nationwide implementation,
continued to view the economic reform with great suspicion.
Antonin Novotny, speaking to the Party Central Committee
Plenum in March, 1967, put it this way: "As long as economic
measures are not in harmony with our political aims and our
political program, these measures cannot be accepted by us,
no matter how effective they may be."[3]

But the public admission by the Party elite of the drama-
tic failure of the socialist economy of Czechoslovakia and its at
least partial acceptance of the economic reform, accompanied
by a nationwide public debate, brought about an almost universal awareness on the part of the population that the Party
was, indeed, wrong in at least some of its decisions on crucial
matters of state and society. An awakening of expectations
that, this being the case, other national reforms should and
perhaps would follow, gripped the nation. The traditional communist mode of decision-making was now officially admitted
to be inadequate. The politically relevant citizens, suddenly
aware of the new, broadening limits, were ready to move from
submission to bargaining. The large and rapid proliferation of
roles, groups and classes, perceived as possible and indeed
feasible under the umbrella of the New Economic Model, made
definite and growing societal aspirations and demands almost
legitimate. The statistical evidence from public opinion polls
and surveys affirmed the general national dissatisfaction and
made it public property.

The hesitant beginning of economic restratification in Czechoslovakia was thus expected to lead to broad social restratification. To start with, it was indeed assumed that those who add significantly to the national product would receive more money with which to buy more and better goods and services—a process leading to formulation of socially differentiated pluralistic groups.[4] And this in a society where excessive egalitarianism and social nonantagonism had been celebrated as the basis of complete political homogeneity.

SOCIAL CHANGES

The second proposition stipulates that different economic organizations call for different social structures. In the new economic arrangement the producers must be rewarded in a currency that would motivate them. This means increasing transformation of the atomized instruments of the former economic organization into stratified validators of the new economic process. Diffusion of choices, differentiation of roles, competition, and upward mobility of the able are the ways by which amorphous masses crystallize and cluster into social groups and classes. And these groups now demand legitimation of both substructural social autonomy and of pluralistic social interests.

Out of the initial and partial economic reforms and the expectations of a better life which they aroused, emerged various competing social and institutional groups, within as well as without the Party. They appealed to different segments of the Party elite for action, and the elite, in turn, ultimately appealed to them for support. These groups may be broadly identified as follows:

1. THE ECONOMIC REFORMERS.

These were the academic economists, principally associated with the Economic Institute of the Academy of Sciences.

They are young, bright, energetic pragmatists whose articulate and professional diagnosis of the economic maladies had forced the harassed Party elite to consider their critical proposals seriously.

2. THE PROFESSIONAL SOCIAL SCIENTISTS.

Social scientists, with their opinion and preference surveys, empirical political and social studies, among other endeavors, were being elevated to a new status, perceived as more appropriate to the new needs, for the Party's own efforts at social engineering were no longer considered as being relevant. The social scientists' recent undisturbed and supported existence within new information structures allowed them to expand and extend their roles. They became an important group because of their unique position of access to data and information otherwise unattainable. in a state where efficiency was the basis of authority. They became barometers of change in a society which only lately had they been permitted to investigate.

3. THE CREATIVE INTELLECTUALS.

Before the 1948 communist coup d'état, the Czechoslovak intellectual elite tended to be left of the center. During the first decade of Communist Party rule, when popular participation in politics sharply subsided, the intellectuals, now in the party, had on the whole supported the regime. Recruitment of cadres to staff the new ruling Party came principally from this group. But in the second decade of Communist Party rule a widening gap appeared between the Party elite and the intellectuals. The Party elite proved unable to put down the rapidly growing criticism of the regime by the intellectuals, and failed to mobilize the support of the masses against the intellectual elite. Thus, the Fourth Congress of the Writers Union in June, 1967, was a climactic affair and one that became a major catalyst of future political development.

Here the irate members of the Congress for the first time attacked the Party leadership publicly and collectively. Said Ludvik Vaculik, a novelist, author of the famous *Two Thousand Words:* "Instead of a resilient cultural community, we have an easily dominated, amorphous human mass whom it is a sheer joy to rule—even for a foreigner." [5] The Congress demanded changes in existing policies and practices. The Party leadership responded with suppression.

4. THE STUDENTS.

In November, 1967, university students in a Prague hostel staged a march through Prague for simple economic reasons; there had been no light or heat in their hostel for months. The police intervened in force. Many students were arrested and beaten, but the police brutality was so widely criticized that the Party agreed to investigate the incident. The result was an unprecedented admission of public mistakes. The date was December 14, 1967.

5. THE SLOVAKS.

The second largest national group in Czechoslovakia, the Slovaks have always occupied an ambiguous position. During the Stalinist period the political, social, and cultural freedoms of the Slovaks, formulated in the 1945 Kosice program, had been gradually curbed by the Party. However, an explosive dichotomy began to appear: while political and social freedoms were disappearing, the economic build-up of underdeveloped Slovakia was proceeding rapidly. The key to solving the nationality problem was considered to be the Stalinist formula of economic equalization between the two dominant subcultures (Czechs and Slovaks).

Nevertheless, since 1963, Slovak intellectuals had more and more openly criticized the centrist policies of the Party. They pointed out that economic growth which is not founded in the subcultural social and political life but rests on the quicksand of political coercion, is both lopsided and artificial. By 1967, the Slovaks became most restive.

6. OTHERS.

The social and cultural groups described above were joined by others demanding substructural autonomy: mass associations such as trade unions and youth organizations; people working in the mass communication media such as the press, radio, and film industry; formerly suppressed and powerless political parties, members of the National Front, both Czech and Slovak; and formerly disbanded organizations like the Boy Scouts and the national athletic association, SOKOL. New organizations such as the Club of Engaged Non-Party People, citizens who wanted to participate actively in the political process; the K 231, a club of victims of the Stalinist terror of the fifties, dedicated to the rehabilitation of former political prisoners; and the Society for Human Rights emerged in the spring of 1968.

These were the major social and institutional groups which appeared or reappeared to represent the new pluralistic social interests.

POLITICAL CHANGES

The third proposition postulates that altered social structures call for different political structures, involving changes in political authority and decision-making. Members of vociferous new social groups have definite and growing aspirations, expectations, and demands, which become political.

What were the major demands made by the new social groups in Czechoslovakia? Some already have been implied: abolition of censorship and freedom of the press; rehabilitation of all victims of the past terror; and a federal system with adequate autonomy for the Slovaks. In addition, the groups now pressed for legal freedom of assembly, freedom of religion, a more active and independent foreign policy (but clearly within the frame of the existing regional arrangements, namely, the Council for Mutual Economic Assistance, the Warsaw Pact, and the close ties with socialist neighbors and the Soviet Union). They asked for freedom to participate in national political life and freedom of elections. The groups and classes did not ask for more decision-making power for more people, but insisted that more people with ideas and information be given both a forum for presenting their ideas, and access to those making the political decisions.[6] They thus collectively demanded things which could not be accommodated within the existing political organization. The new social groups forced the Party elite to rethink the basic political question: What is the role of the Party in the present stage of socioeconomic development in Czechoslovakia? The Party conservatives, understandably, wished to return, with minor concessions, to the past of absolute Party control. The Party conservatives, understandably, wished to return, with establishment of "friendly socialist opposition parties," namely, genuinely political opposition parties within a socialist democracy. Those in between, the Centrists, demanded that the Party democratize its own structures, permit expression of minority views, introduce internal differentiation, and engage in a public dialogue within the Party community and thus prove that it deserves to survive as a monopoly party.

The Party of Novotny could not even begin to cope with political debates and demands such as these. This is when Novotny's usefulness ended—when he failed to realize that he could not deal with demands by relying on the simple and simplistic political coercion used in the past. (I would flatter Mr. Novotny if I said that he certainly was not the man for all seasons.)

Alexander Dubcek saw that the new political aspirations were legitimate and could no longer be handled within existing political structures. Changes which had to be made in the political organization to accommodate these demands would affect political authority in Czechoslovakia. Public discussion of these issues signaled the breakdown of the unanimity model in the public policy-making of the past, and also the beginning of a new political era, an era of the creative development of a socialism which would be capable of accommodating democracy. The discussion on what was essential to the new national political life took place in the spring and summer of 1968. The threat to political authority led to the Soviet intervention in August.

FOREIGN REACTION TO DOMESTIC CHANGES

The last proposition is that a domestic change has foreign ramifications that may in turn dominate it.

East European Party elites must be viewed as having two major validators: the constituents at home and the organizer and coalition leader, the USSR, abroad.[7] In the "command stage" of economic development, the chances that the Party leaders will stay in office may be calculated simply by judging the extent to which domestic goals attained are considered desirable by the USSR. As long as the East European Parties faithfully follow Soviet wishes, all is well.

As the economy develops further, however, and changes have taken place in the economic, social, and political structures, the chances that the Party leaders will stay in office must be calculated increasingly by judging the extent to which the domestic goals attained are considered desirable by the constituents. The wishes, aspirations, and demands of the citizens now become much more important than before. But the chances of pleasing the two validators, the domestic constituency and the Soviet Union, are inversely related. The more the leaders satisfy the citizens, the less they satisfy the USSR. By making substantial concessions to Czechoslovak social groups, the Czechoslovak Party decreased its tribute to the USSR. The political consequences of the new social complexity in Czechoslovakia were perceived by at least some of the Soviet decision-makers as a dangerous decrease in the degree of Czechoslovak solidarity with the USSR. The result was the Soviet intervention.

The rivalry between two types of validators was ex-

acerbated by the needs of national identity. James Billington
was correct in noting "a separate [national] identity and [a
separate national] development is a [necessary] prerequisite
to full and dignified participation" in any political system,
national or international.[8] Billington compares this search for
separate national identity and tendency to return to national
traditions in Eastern Europe with a similar search and
tendency among the advocates of Black Power in the United
States today. The Czechs and Slovaks indeed have this shared
feeling that they have been treated as "semicolonial, faintly
inferior, and—worst of all—historically irrelevant second-
class" citizens.

In the formation of political attitudes, development and
maintenance of national identity is of vital importance. Social
psychologists, in their studies of the psychology of identity,[9]
and political scientists, in treating political development,[10]
agree that when national identity is in question, a frantic
search for restored identity begins. The psychology of identity
certainly provides "a clue to the tenacity of national
attachment."

Deutsch, Russet, and others confirm this finding,[11] pointing out that successful international systems have stopped
short of total integration and have accommodated autonomous
national units. In other words, the integration capacity of international systems is limited by the autonomy of national
units as well as by the kind of national identity within them.
If these units are in flux, the international system is bound to
be unstable.[12] Thus a stable Eastern Europe depends on the
existence of stable separate national identities. The Soviet intervention in Czechoslovakia was a move to preserve integration in Eastern Europe.

But it had the opposite effect. Soviet intervention de-
stabilized both Czechoslovakia and Eastern Europe. Czechoslovakia became visibly, and the other East European states
under the surface, less securely attached to the Soviet socialist
community. The East European integration is being preserved
at the expense of perpetuating and deepening the fundamental
identity crisis in Eastern Europe. If the Soviet Union wished
to create a stable, supranational community in Eastern Europe,

then its invasion of Czechoslovakia was a terrible mistake. If it wished merely to preserve and strengthen its own protective wall on its western border, namely to place Soviet tanks as close to Germany and Austria as possible, then the occupation was the most clumsy way to do it. In either case, it was short-sighted for the Soviets to view Czechoslovak improvements of early 1968 as their loss. Long-term stability and settlement in Eastern Europe suffered great harm.

The Soviet Union also had its validators, pushing it to intervention. As the organizer it is also the captive of its alliance system; the legitimation-socialization process works both ways. The possibility of being charged with condoning revisionism and with alienation from socialism, not only by the Chinese but also by less critical allies, undoubtedly helps the Soviet leaders to toe the line. Their freedom of maneuver is limited by their socialist allies, who are the external valida-tors of their legitimacy. The external pressure upon the Soviet leaders to cope with the Czechoslovak situation must have played a significant role in the Soviet decision to intervene.

Moreover, domestic demands for social and political change in Eastern Europe are not really understood in the Soviet Union. Although the East European countries differ a great deal from each other, all are even more different from the Soviet Union. Their party bureaucracies are less firmly established, less autonomous, and less pressure-resistant than the strong Soviet Party bureaucracy; people who once lived under multiparty rule in the not too distant past are still alive, and have not forgotten the traditions of at least a cer-tain amount of political freedom. Many long to rejoin the West, for the consumer values of the West are widely admired. The level of consumption has improved over the past two to three decades in Russia, but not in the satellites. Religious ties, thought limited, have survived. Furthermore, Soviet techno-cratic elites, created and supported by the Party, are dependent on and even proud of their affiliation with the CPSU, whereas East European technocrats and professionals—alienated, eco-nomically suppressed, and socially and politically discrim-inated against by their parties—feel differently, whether they are Party members or not. As a consequence, the demands for change—and the elites' potential political responsiveness—are considerably greater in the small East European countries than in the Soviet Union.

I have argued that modernization determines the nature of political authority, that is, that the social consequences of the functional requisites of the new economic stages call for changes in the structure of authority and decision-making. This argument does not go so far as the hypothesis of Seymour Lipset and others, who stipulate that increase in modernization increases democracy.[13] But my point is that neither construct is valid unless the intervening variable of foreign influence and ties is calculated and incorporated into the hypothesis. No political system is an island unto itself. East European countries, and now Czechoslovakia in particular, illustrate this point.

NOTES

1. This is a short version of a more comprehensive study which is based on extensive interviews in Czechoslovakia and Poland, East Germany, Hungary, Yugoslavia, Romania, and Bulgaria during the academic year 1966–1967 and again in Czechoslovakia in the late summer of 1968. I am grateful to the American Philosophical Society for the generous grant which made my field research possible.

2. *See* Ota Sik, *K Problematice socialistickych zboznich bztahu.* (*The Problems of Commodity Relations in a Socialist Economy*), (Prague: Ceskoslovenská Akademie Ved, 1967), esp. Part II.

3. *Rudé právö*, March 30, 1967, p. 1.

4. Emil Durkheim, *The Division of Labor* (Glencoe, Ill.: Free Press of Glencoe, 1949), *passim*.

5. *IV Sjezd Svazu Ceskoslo-*

venskych Spisovatelu (Praha: Ceskoslovensky spisovatel, 1968), p. 141.

6. James Bourgart in a research memo to the author, Stanford, Institute of Political Studies, Fall, 1968.

7. This discussion is based on Harold Guetzkow's "Structured Programs and their Relation to Free Activity within the Inter-Nation Simulation" in *Simulation in International Relations: Developments for Research and Teaching* (Englewood Cliffs, N.J.: Prentice-Hall, 1963), pp. 110–15.

8. James H. Billington, "Force and Counterforce in Eastern Europe," *Foreign Affairs*, XLVII, No. 1 (October, 1968), 31.

9. Erik H. Erikson, *Childhood and Society* (New York: Norton, 1950); Leonard Doob, *Patriotism and Nationalism: Their Psycho-*

logical Foundations (New Haven: Yale Univ. Press, 1965).

10. Lucien Pye, *Politics, Personality, and Nation Building* (New Haven, Yale Univ. Press, 1962); Sidney Verba and Lucian Pye, *Comparative Political Culture* (Princeton: Princeton Univ. Press, 1965).

11. Karl W. Deutsch, *Political Community at the International Level* (New York: Doubleday, 1954); Bruce M. Russett, *Community and Contention: Britain and America in the Twentieth Century* (Cambridge, Mass.: M.I.T. Press, 1963).

12. Bruce Sievers, *The Divided Nations: International Integration and National Identity* (Stanford University Studies of the Commu-

nist System, 1966), mimeo., p. 30.

13. Seymour M. Lipset, *Political Man* (Garden City, N.Y.: Doubleday, 1960); Karl W. Deutsch, "Social Mobilization and Political Development," *Am. Poli. Sci. Rev.* (Sept. 1961), pp. 493–514; Daniel Lerner, *The Passing of Traditional Society* (New York: Free Press of Glencoe, 1958); David E. Apter, *The Politics of Modernization* (Chicago and London: Univ. of Chicago Press, 1965); Gabriel A. Almond and James S. Coleman (eds.), *The Politics of the Developing Areas* (Princeton: Princeton Univ. Press, 1960), pp. 17–26; Bruce M. Russett *et al.*, *World Handbook of Political and Social Indicators* (New Haven: Yale Univ. Press, 1964), pp. 261ff.

The Soviet Union and Eastern Europe: The Aftermath of the Czechoslovak Invasion

by Vernon V. Aspaturian

The brutal Soviet occupation of Communist Czechoslovakia in August, 1968, on the 30th anniversary of Munich and the 20th anniversary of the internal Communist Party coup of 1948 signals an ominous turn in Soviet relationships with Eastern Europe, whose full implications for internal Soviet developments, Sino-Soviet relations, the world Communist movement, East-West relations, and particularly for Soviet-American relations are as yet not fully predictable. There is little question but that all of these relationships will undergo multiple reexamination and change.

Not only has the Soviet occupation of Czechoslovakia reversed a welcome tendency on the part of the Soviet leaders in exercising self-restraint in their dealings with Moscow's former vassal states, but it also calls into question the internal political stability, judgment and even basic honesty of the Soviet regime in its dealings with other countries. The circumstances of the Soviet occupation, coming as it did so soon after the Cierna and Bratislava meetings between the Soviet and Czech hierarchies, is bound to raise once again the entire

15

question of the role of duplicity as a conscious and calculated instrument of Soviet diplomacy.[1]

The 1968 subjugation of Czechoslovakia signifies therefore a new phase in the evolving relationship between Moscow and the states of Eastern Europe—a phase in which the naked security and national interests of the Soviet Union are unambiguously given a higher priority than ideological considerations. Whatever the ideological rationalizations used to justify intervention in Czech affairs they were only routinely and cursorily invoked and failed to persuade most of the Communist Parties of the world. The Soviet action provoked condemnation by China, Rumania, Yugoslavia, and Albania, among Communist countries and denunciation by the leadership of the French and Italian Communist Parties. The flimsiness of Moscow's ideological pretext was further exposed by the Poles' frank admission that they cooperated in the venture on grounds of *raison d'état*—surely as distant from the cherished Marxist-Leninist principle of "proletarian internationalism" as one can visualize.

In subordinating ideological interests, norms, and goals to Soviet state interests, needs, and requirements, the Soviet Union not only has tended to confirm Peking's charge that Moscow's behavior is solely determined by the interests of the Soviet "revisionist clique," but by its outrageous violation of the principle of "proletarian internationalism," the Soviet Union has also subverted whatever remained of the underlying theoretical basis of the world Communist movement and system.

The Soviet action has seriously risked, *inter alia*, the following hazards and dangers as well to its position in world affairs:

1. The further disorientation and division of the world communist movement.
2. The weakening of Communist Parties in non-communist countries and the erosion of their electoral support, particularly in France, Italy, and India.
3. The further disorganization and fracturing of the Communist bloc into factional and hostile groupings, particularly in Eastern Europe.

4. The tarnishing of its carefully cultivated image as a mature and responsible global power that exercised its enormous power with consummate self-restraint and prudence.
5. The exposure of its government as a blatant violator of the elemental norms of international law (nonintervention, noninterference, independence and sovereignty) which Moscow has repeatedly proclaimed before various forums as sacrosanct.
6. The revelation that Russia has little concern for "world public opinion."
7. The threat to a Soviet-American detente by jeopardizing Senate ratification of the non-proliferation treaty and providing Bonn with a credible justification for refusing to accede to it, by arousing and encouraging the "hard-liners" in the United States and risking the revitalization of NATO as well as assuring that there would be little or no withdrawal of United States troops from Europe.
8. The provision of precedent and justification for the intervention of the United States and other great powers in the affairs of smaller states.

There is little reason to doubt that the Soviet leaders understood the grave risks that they were taking, and we must assume that the action was conscious and deliberate, even though it may have been taken after acrimonious and bitter controversy and probably against the better judgment of a substantial segment of the Soviet leadership. Why? The indications are that once again the interests of the Soviet Union as the leader of a revolutionary movement and the interests of the Soviet Union as a state had come into contradiction and that one set of interests had to be subordinated to the other.[2] This has frequently happened in the past and the resolution has nearly always been in favor of Soviet state interests.

What makes this particular action unique, however, is the fact that the Soviet leaders were unable to correlate and identify their state interests with ideology in such a way to persuade most Communists throughout the world.[3] Even Fidel Castro was moved to concede that the Soviet action was illegal, immoral, and contrary to basic Communist precepts, but he nevertheless supported it on grounds of Cuban self-interest. Significantly, support for the Soviet action came only from those parties and states (Communist and non-Communist) that perceived it to be in their self-interest.

When the Soviet Union established its sphere of influence in Eastern Europe after World War II, Soviet state and ideological interests were conveniently and logically in agreement. The establishment of a Soviet bloc simultaneously satisfied Russia's historic and strategic need for a security belt and a springboard to the further communization of Europe.

Increasingly, however, these two purposes for Soviet presence in Eastern Europe have been rendered incompatible, as the Soviet role and position in the international Communist movement has been challenged from within and eroded by the obstacles and hazards from without. By resorting to the military occupation of Czechoslovakia, the Soviet leaders have indicated their determination to maintain a sphere of influence in the traditional great power sense and have thereby simultaneously implied that the Eastern European countries, for all practical purposes, can no longer serve as a springboard for the further communization of Europe.

The occupation of Czechoslovakia by the military forces of the Soviet Union and four of its Warsaw Pact allies thus inaugurates the latest phase in the evolution of a relationship between Moscow and Eastern Europe that has gone through several distinct phases of development during the past half-century.[4]

HISTORY AND GEOGRAPHY

The relationship between the Soviet Union and Eastern Europe which emerged after World War II was shaped by a complex of factors which almost defy comprehensive analysis. History, geography, culture, language, religion, psychological attachments, national character, and ideology have all influenced the development of the relationship, although the impact of each factor has varied considerably with the individual countries of Eastern Europe. In each case, the particular complex has in turn contributed to determining relations between Moscow and the different countries of Eastern Europe. Thus, some of these factors have served to bind the countries of Eastern Europe to Moscow, while others have served to alienate them. It is not always a simple matter to sort out and disentagle the contradictory and converging forces which shape the attitudes of individual countries to the Soviet Union.

Consideration of history and geography alone would appear sufficient to explain the special role for Moscow in this region. Geographically, the area has been a buffer zone between Russia and other major powers of central Europe for many centuries, and, for the past two hundred years, Russia has sought to assert a dominant influence in the region. Yet the specific character and form of the subordination suggest that other factors have been equally influential.

Many of the Eastern European attitudes and perceptions were shaped by the events and circumstances of nineteenth-century European diplomacy. Less than two hundred years ago, all of the nationalities of Eastern Europe (except the Serbs of Montenegro) were languishing under Ottoman or Hapsburg domination. The circumstances of their liberation and independence were to shape national attitudes toward Russia for many decades.

Since all of the subject nationalities of the Ottoman and Hapsburg Empires in the region were either Slavic and/or Orthodox (with the exception of the Magyars who became a co-ruling nationality in 1848), the fact that Russia was the largest and most powerful Slavic and Orthodox state was destined to influence both Russia's diplomatic calculations and Eastern Europe's perceptions. Russia was instrumental in liberating the Rumanians, Bulgars, and Serbs and was eager to pose as the champion and potential deliverer of the Croats, Slovenes, Czechs, and Slovaks (all Catholic but Slavic) from Hapsburg domination. Thus was forged a symbiotic relationship between Russia and the Slavic/Orthodox nationalities of Eastern Europe, which was manifested before World War I in the Pan-Slavic movement that has in many ways survived the vicissitudes of revolutionary upheaval, social convulsions, elite hostilities, military occupation, territorial dismemberment, political subjugation, ideological conflict, and two world wars. The Rumanians, being Orthodox but non-Slavic, have

conflicting perceptions, for, while Russia was instrumental
in freeing them from Ottoman rule, Moscow has insisted upon
retaining Bessarabia, considered part of Rumania *irredenta*.
Hungary and Poland have traditionally viewed Russia both as
a rival for power in the region and as an oppressor. This is
particularly true of Poland, a Catholic Slavic nation, with its
own proud history as a great power in the area, the bulk of
whose population languished under Russian rule and oppression for over a century.

The complex and interesting ethnic, religious, political,
geographic and historical variables which have contributed
to the shaping of Eastern European attitudes towards the
Soviet Union can be summarized by the following chart:

THE EFFECTS OF COMMUNISM

While both history and geography impelled the Soviet
Union to assert its dominance and influence in Eastern Europe,
an explanation of the precise nature of the current relationship is to be found in relations between the Communist Party
of the Soviet Union and the world Communist movement, of
which the Eastern European Communist Parties were an in-
tegral part before the Second World War.

The entire history of the Soviet relationships with foreign
Communist Parties, with Communist states, and then with
rivals for Communist leadership (China), has been dominated by two essentially contradictory criteria: the interests
of foreign constituencies (world revolution, party-states,
China), or the interests of internal constituencies (survival as
a state, national interests, Soviet elites).

Tension between these two conflicting sets of demands is
inevitable, for they are not easily reconciled. One is bound to
subordinate the other; either the Soviet state must become
an expendable instrument of the international proletariat or
the Communist movement must be subjugated to the demands
of the Soviet state. This contradiction has been resolved in
the past by adjusting the interests and behavior of foreign
Communist Parties to those of the Soviet state, and from 1928

CHART I

Variables and Factors Shaping Eastern European Images and Attitudes Towards the U.S.S.R.

COUNTRY	POSITIVE							NEGATIVE								IDEOLOGICAL					
	Slavic	Orthodox	Russia viewed as liberator	Friendly dynasty before World War I	Allied State, World War I	Allied State, World War II	Amicable official relations before World War II	Non-Slavic	Non-Orthodox	Russia viewed as enemy or oppressor	Hostile dynasty before World War I	Enemy State, World War I	Hostile official relations before World War II	Enemy State, World War II	Territorial conflict with Russia/U.S.S.R.	Soviet Military Occupation	Strong Communist Party before World War II	Strong Guerrilla Movement	Warsaw Pact	CEMA	Support Moscow over Peking
Albania		X[1]						X	X[1]				X	X				X	X[2]	X[2]	
Bulgaria	X	X	X[5]									X	X			X			X	X	X
Czechoslovakia	X		X			X	X		X			X[4]			X[3]				X	X	X
East Germany							X	X	X		X	X	X	X		X	X		X	X	X
Hungary								X	X	X	X	X	X	X	X	X			X	X	X
Poland	X					X			X	X	X		X		X	X			X	X	X
Rumania		X			X			X		X	X			X	X	X			X	X	X
Yugoslavia	X	X[1]	X	X[6]	X[6]	X							X					X			X

1. Orthodox; Catholic; and Moslem.
2. Not active since 1962; withdrew from the Warsaw Pact on September 13, 1968.
3. Carpatho-Ukraine was part of Hungary before World War I and between March 1939 and 1944.
4. As far as Russia was concerned.
5. Ambivalent; negative image since late 19th century.
6. Serbia and Montenegro.

to 1953, foreign Communist Parties, even after they assumed power in their own countries, remained instruments rather than partners of the Soviet Union.

Until the installation of Communist regimes in the countries of Eastern Europe, the Soviet Union had a unique position as the only Communist state in the world, whose ruling proletariat preempted the articulation of the class interests of the entire world proletariat languishing in oppression and exploitation in capitalist countries. As long as the Soviet Union was the only Communist state, it could be rationalized that good Communists everywhere should display first loyalty to the only fatherland of the proletariat. Loyalty, however, was not founded on the inherent moral superiority or priority of interests of the Soviet proletariat over all others, but on the basis that as the only country ruled by a proletariat, class interests dictated highest loyalty to the base and center of the world revolutionary movement, a principle known as "proletarian internationalism." The international proletariat gave its loyalty to the Soviet Union on the premise that the Soviet Union was the only authentic representative of the class interests of proletarians in all countries. That it was the Russian proletariat which ruled the first Communist state was simply a function of historical fortuity, and legitimized neither its moral nor political superiority.

Proletarian internationalism became, in effect, a device for converting party subservience into state vassalage. Entire countries were subjugated and their interests subordinated to that of the Russianized Soviet state. Some satellite leaders, however, demurred and interpreted the Stalinist theory of "proletarian internationalism" as applicable only to Parties in capitalist countries; otherwise it became a philosophical justification for Soviet imperialism and colonialism. The refusal of Tito and other satellite leaders to place the interests of the Soviet state above their own and to act as Moscow's subservient agents of plunder and exploitation in the name of "proletarian internationalism," resulted in Tito's expulsion and the wholesale liquidation of satellite leaders who betrayed signs of wavering loyalty.

When Stalin died in March, 1953, the dominance of the

Soviet Union in the Communist system appeared fixed and permanent and the primacy of its interests established and assured. Stalin's death, however, unleashed internal divisions among his successors, and this created opportunities for other Communist states to stir and come back to life. Amorphous factional groupings assumed shape in satellite capitals corresponding to those in the Kremlin. The more inconclusive the struggle in Moscow, the greater the apprehension in Eastern Europe. Direction from Moscow became contradictory, inconsistent, wavering and hesitant. Surviving anti-Stalinists in satellite countries challenged their own Stalinist leaders, awash in the wake of Soviet confusion. As the internal controversy became more acute, uncertain, and incapacitating, Kremlin factions reached into the empire for incremental support. Communist leaders were once again about to become power constituencies.

First Peking in 1954, then Yugoslavia in 1955, and Poland in 1956, made demands upon the Soviet Union which were met and have since been granted to other Communist states. The demands of the Nagy regime in Hungary were such that they could be met only at the risk of permitting the system to disintegrate; they were forcibly denied. By 1958, the Soviet Union was bombarded with demands, trivial and serious, from all directions. While Moscow continued to make its own demands upon other Communist states, they were more limited and less coercively executed. The balance in the flow of demands, however, was radically upset during the years 1957-1961, as demands flowing in from the periphery gradually exceeded those flowing outward from the center.

As the Eastern European states continued to assert the priority of their own national interests in one area after another in their dealings with the USSR, it was virtually axiomatic that, as they succeeded in resisting or trimming the demands made upon them by Moscow, they would reverse the flow of demands. The Council of Mutual Economic Assistance (Comecon), for example, which was originally conceived to facilitate the economic plundering of Eastern Europe by Moscow, was reorganized to control and arrest Soviet exploitation. No sooner had this happened, than it was converted into

a vehicle for draining economic resources from the Soviet
Union to the Eastern European countries, as demands were
made in Moscow for restitution, reparations, economic assistance, and commercial autonomy. The Eastern European states
asserted the right to receive economic assistance from and
engage in profitable commercial transactions with capitalist
countries.

Economic demands upon the Soviet Union spilled over
into the political and ideological realms, as individual states
demanded and received greater internal autonomy. Soviet-
modeled institutions were, in many cases, dissolved or modified. Soviet-type ideological controls over the arts, sciences,
professions, education and information media were renounced
in accordance with the local demands of each state. The Comin-
form itself was abolished in response to these demands.

The extent to which demands were successfully asserted
depended in large measure upon the power of each individual
state, for no overt attempt was made to organize joint or con-
certed action in making demands upon Moscow until 1961,
when China and Albania forged an anti-Soviet factional alliance. Up to that time, only the Soviet Union could mobilize
other Parties and states against another member of the
Communist confraternity.

The 20th Party Congress constitutes a major watershed
in the evolution of Soviet relations with the rest of the Communist world. Locally responsive Communists like Gomulka
and Nagy were catapulted into power in Poland and Hungary
by powerful internal pressures which were set into motion by
the revelations of the 20th Party Congress. The demolition of
Stalinism at home could only result in the progressive disintegration of Stalinist structures in Eastern Europe, which
had been erected in response to the dictates of Moscow. The
internal effects of destalinization in China, Yugoslavia, and
Albania, however, were minimal, for these countries were
governed largely by indigenous Stalinist or already destalin-
ized regimes. The Polish and Hungarian "Octobers" were the
immediate and most serious consequences of destalinization,
and the demands both events placed upon the Communist system threatened to reduce it to ruins. The nationalism of both

the Soviets and the smaller satellites could no longer be obscured by the smokescreen of proletarian internationalism. The year 1956 thus inaugurated the gradual dissolution of proletarian internationalism into its constituent proletarian or Communist nationalisms.

While it was Tito's defection in 1948 that pointed the way, Stalin's death in 1953 that created the opportunity, and the 20th Party Congress that gave initial impetus to pluralistic communism, it was the Sino-Soviet split, the detente with the United States (as a consequence of the partial nuclear test ban treaty signed in July, 1963), and Khrushchev's sudden and unceremonious ouster in October 1964, that created new opportunities and successively accelerated the fragmentation of the Communist bloc and the liberalization of internal regimes. The Sino-Soviet conflict enabled the smaller states of Eastern Europe to play off the two Communist giants against one another and thus afforded them the opportunity to develop greater autonomy *within* the Communist movement as both Peking and Moscow bid for their favor and support. First Albania succeeded in using China to separate herself from Soviet paternalism and then Rumania offered herself as a "neutral" mediator between Russia and China while simultaneously enlarging her own freedom of action.

The Test Ban Treaty of July 1963 and the Soviet-American detente provided the further opportunity to expand freedom of action outside the Communist world. The Soviet-American detente served to diminish both the U.S. threat to Moscow and the Soviet threat to the West and thus contributed to the progressive erosion of both NATO and the Warsaw Treaty Organization. The expansion of internal autonomy spilled over in the realm of foreign policy when Rumania, in April 1964, announced a virtual declaration of independence, refusing to subordinate its economic development to the central coordination and planning of Comecon and to accept its dictate to concentrate on agricultural development and spurn industrialization.[5]

After Khrushchev's ouster, Rumania refused to accept a Soviet demand that all Warsaw Pact countries adopt uniform rules on military conscription; instead, it reduced the military obligation of its conscriptees to below the suggested level. In 1966, Rumania issued its first independent call for the dissolution of all military blocs and in the same year demanded that Moscow not employ nuclear weapons without consulting the other members of the Warsaw Treaty Organization. At the same time, Bucharest questioned the right of Moscow to select the commander of the Warsaw Treaty forces and suggested that it be rotated among the other members.[6] The same year Rumania concluded important commercial arrangements with Western countries, thus reducing her trade with the Soviet Union to about 30 percent of the total by 1968 and further restricting Moscow's capability to take punitive action. Since 1964, Rumanian leaders have refused to condemn Red China and side with Moscow in the Sino-Soviet split and have adopted a policy of pursuing friendly relations with *all* countries, including the United States. In apparent pursuance of this policy, Rumania served as a diplomatic conduit between Washington and Hanoi, established normal diplomatic relations with West Germany, refused to condemn Israel as the aggressor in the June 1967 Arab-Israeli war and continued to maintain diplomatic relations with Israel, received the only visit of an American president to a Communist country, and voted independently of the Soviet bloc on a number of issues in the U.N.

During the first half of 1968, Rumania's defiance of the Soviet Union accelerated and was no doubt encouraged by developments in Prague. As the Czechs expanded their area of internal freedom, Bucharest expanded hers in foreign policy and the two processes appeared to feed back and forth upon one another. Thus, beginning on March 1968, Rumania withdrew from the Budapest Consultative Conference of Communist Parties, and a week later at the Sofia meeting of the Warsaw Pact powers, refused to sign the "unanimous" declaration endorsing the draft non-proliferation treaty sponsored by Moscow and Washington, on the grounds that it represented another infringement on the sovereignty of the smaller non-nuclear powers by Russia and America. It was the first time that a document of this character was issued without the signature of all the members of the Warsaw Pact, although the meeting was sufficiently important to attract the Party heads, foreign ministers and defense ministers of all seven allied powers.[7]

This was followed by Bucharest's refusal to participate in the Dresden Conference of Warsaw Powers and its crude threat to intervene in Czechoslovakia (March 23-24, 1968). Rumania similarly refused (as did Czechoslovakia) to participate in the Warsaw meeting of the alliance on July 14-15, 1968, which issued an even more threatening ultimatum to the Dubcek regime, while Warsaw Pact forces were deliberately delaying their departure from Czech territory although their summer military exercises (which Rumania refused to join) had been completed. During this period, Rumanian leaders publicly encouraged the Czech reformers and at the height of the crisis, President Ceausescu offered to lend his personal presence in Prague in a joint gesture of defiance. Dubcek prudently declined the offer, but after the Cierna and Bratislava meetings with the Soviet leadership, Ceausescu followed Tito to Prague in a display of solidarity. To Moscow, it would seem that the pre-war Little Entente was being resurrected as a hostile grouping in its erstwhile placid garden of client and vassal states. After the Soviet intervention, Rumania continued its gestures of defiance: it condemned the invasion, demanded that all Communist states be masters of their own affairs, vowed never to allow Warsaw Pact forces on Soviet territory, placed the entire country on the alert, and threatened to actively resist any possible Soviet encroachment on its sovereignty.

DESATELLITIZATION AND DESTALINIZATION

Before the Czech invasion, the countries of Eastern Europe could be divided into four distinct categories in reference to their relationship to the Soviet Union: (1) Yugoslavia, an independent, virtually "neutralist" and "nonaligned" Communist state that exercised complete sovereignty over its domestic and foreign policy; (2) Albania, an independent, anti-

Soviet (antirevisionist) Communist state, ideologically allied
with but not under the control of China or any other Communist state; (3) the Warsaw Pact countries of Poland, Czechoslovakia, Bulgaria, East Germany, and Hungary, residual satellite—more properly client—states of Moscow;[8] and (4) Rumania, a dissident and noncooperative member of the Warsaw
Pact and Comecon, "neutral" in the Sino-Soviet conflict, and
quasi-independent in its foreign policy. After the Czech invasion, both Yugoslavia and Rumania were further alienated
from Moscow and the bloc; Czechoslovakia was returned to
vassalage; and Poland was forced into greater dependence
on the Soviet Union and was threatened with *de facto* diplomatic isolation.

The current diversity in Eastern Europe is the consequence of two distinct but closely interrelated processes: destalinization and desatellitization.[9] Destalinization refers primarily to the dismantling of Stalinist institutions and practices in domestic life, and in the beginning closely followed the
destalinization taking place in Russia itself. Desatellitization
refers to the process whereby the individual countries of
Eastern Europe gradually reasserted their autonomy and independence from Soviet control, a process that is still continuing. Desatellitization has been a universal phenomenon,
whereas destalinization has not. At a certain stage of development the two processes came into conflict, since some countries
asserted their independence in order to retain certain Stalinist
institutions and norms or to resist their complete dismantling.
In Albania, for example, desatellization has resulted in intensification of Stalinist norms rather than greater internal
liberalization. Destalinization was also resisted in varying
degrees in Rumania, Bulgaria and Czechoslovakia as well,
although Stalinism had recently been almost completely re-
pudiated in Czechoslovakia. Destalinization is, in effect, a process of internal liberalization, a process that has progressed at
varying tempos in Eastern Europe, sometimes faster and sometimes slower than in the Soviet Union itself. The two most
independent countries of Eastern Europe reflect opposite
tendencies with reference to Stalinism, with Yugoslavia the

most distant in its departure from Stalinism and Albania the least.

Among the third category (Warsaw Pact) states, Bulgaria remains a tightly run oligarchical state, while Hungary, Poland and Czechoslovakia show varying degrees of liberalization. Poland initially was the boldest in its liberalization, but it soon relinquished its lead to Hungary, whose liberalization continues in spite of the presence of Soviet troops. With the displacement of Antonin Novotny as Secretary-General of the Czech Communist Party by Alexander Dubcek in January 1968, the stage was set for perhaps the most thorough-going liberalization in all Eastern Europe. Czechoslovakia is the only country in the region with a genuine democratic heritage and it was quite possible that Prague may have actually developed into an authentic communist democratic state had not Moscow intervened. Bulgaria, the most pro-Russian and pro-Soviet country (regime and population) in Eastern Europe, closely patterns itself on the Soviet Union.[11]

The terms "destalinization" and "desatellitization" are no longer sufficient to describe the manifold transformations taking place in Eastern Europe. In the case of destalinization, the process had moved into the phase of de-sovietization in some countries and could eventuate even in decommunization, whereas desatellitization might logically result not only in withdrawal from the Soviet alliance and neutralization, but eventually culminate in a reversal of alliances. Either development would affect the balance of power between East and West and both taken together could alter the balance irreversibly. All of these fears and hazards, which were repeatedly expressed by Moscow, Warsaw and Pankow, congealed to trigger the Soviet occupation of Czechoslovakia.

It is not always easy to determine which of the two processes—internal autonomy or independence in foreign policy— is perceived by the Soviet leadership as posing the greatest danger to its interests. Undoubtedly the Soviet leaders are sharply divided on this point, as they are on many others, and the relative danger of the threat of each process varies over time and from one country to another. The Soviet leadership might thus tolerate varying degrees of autonomy and independence, which would in turn depend upon their perception of the strategic importance of the country concerned or the reliability and prudence of its leadership, which further involves an intuitive calculation of the historical images of Russia prevailing in each country. The two processes pose distinct, unrelated sets of dangers and risks for Moscow, which seem to coincide not only with the two main purposes of the Soviet presence in Eastern Europe but also with the two major factional cleavages in the Soviet leadership. Thus growing internal autonomy directly challenges the ideological values and norms of the Soviet system and indirectly the security of the Soviet state, while independence in foreign policy directly erodes Soviet power in world affairs and indirectly constitutes a challenge to Soviet ideological goals and values. Concomitantly, some Soviet leaders, especially those that are ideologically conservative, are more likely to be disturbed by deviations and departures from the Soviet system, while others might be agitated more by the degree of independence asserted in foreign policy, and still others might find both processes equally unpalatable and any combination of the two downright intolerable. Aside from factors such as inertia, factional paralysis, and the impact of cumulative developments, these conflicting perceptions of the "main" danger may account for the extraordinary self-restraint exercised by Moscow towards Rumania's growing independence in foreign policy and her intolerance of developments in Czechoslovakia.

While the Soviet leaders have accommodated and adjusted to the impulse of the Eastern European states to manage their own affairs, as long as they remain "socialist," the absence of any common or universal criteria of what constitutes "socialism" since Khrushchev's denunciation of Stalin in 1956, creates a wide area of ambiguity which causes anxiety in Moscow and inspires boldness and innovation in Eastern European capitals. What started out as "destalinization" in Czechoslovakia was soon legitimized in the doctrine of "separate roads to socialism," but it quickly became evident that the "separate roads" doctrine created both logical possibilities and practical opportunities for subverting and displacing the social orders inspired and established by the Soviet Union. Thus was born the Soviet equivalent of the "falling dominoes" theory. De-stalinization leads to "separate roads," which proliferate into various "national deviations," which may in turn inspire "modern revisionism," which is but a prelude to "social democracy" that quickly degenerates into "bourgeois democracy" and the "restoration of capitalism," [12] which Russia cannot tolerate in Czechoslovakia or anywhere else.

THE THRESHOLD OF INTERVENTION

At what point in the process described by the "Soviet dominoes theory" is Russia likely to intervene? On the surface, it might appear that the threshold in the Czechoslovak case was reached at a point somewhere between "modern revisionism" and "social democracy." In concrete terms, the Soviet Union will intervene when the following developments take place:

1. All censorship, restraints, and sanctions on freedom of expression in the press, arts, and sciences are removed, and freedom of expression and assembly are generally restored.[13]
2. Pressures develop for the restoration of a multiparty system that would jeopardize the political monopoly and control of the Communist Party.[14]
3. Economic innovations are planned that would seriously dilute the "socialist" character of the economic order, returning some sectors of the economy to private hands and allowing a greater latitude for the further expansion of the private sector.
4. Parliamentary government is restored, the power, responsibility, and accountability of which would be to the electorate rather than the Communist Party.

The internal changes that took place in Czechoslovakia

alone, however, were not sufficient in themselves to provoke
Soviet intervention, given the grave risks and costs that such
intervention entail. If these developments could be *contained*
and *restricted* only to Czechoslovakia, then intervention might
have been averted. It appears that it was precisely this assurance that Dubcek and his reformist colleagues gave to Moscow
and that the Soviet leaders initially accepted. On further reflection, however, the Russians judged that Dubcek was either
unwilling or incapable of controlling the situation at home
and certainly unable to prevent the contagion of liberalization
from spreading across Czech frontiers.[15]

Thus, if the infection could not be isolated, then one
might conclude that it was the danger of contagion rather than
the infection alone that was considered the graver risk. Once
Czech liberalization was legitimized by accepting it as a
bona fide variant of Marxism-Leninism, then it would be legitimate for Communists and others to demand the same measures in other communist countries, particularly in Poland,
East Germany and in the Soviet Union itself. Internal dominoes falling in Czechoslovakia alone was bad enough but
might be tolerated, but apparently dominoes falling all over
in Eastern Europe and in the Soviet Union was too much.
Too many vested interests and cherished goals and values
were involved.

The Soviet fear of the consequences of both processes was
first formally registered in the Dresden Conference warning
to Dubcek [16] that events inside Czechoslovakia were threatening the stability and endangering the security of other communist states and then formalized more specifically as an explicit threat to intervene in the Warsaw Powers' statement of
July 15, 1968:

> We cannot agree to have hostile forces push your country from
> the road of Socialism and create a threat of severing Czecho-
> slovakia from the Socialist community, that is something more
> than your cause. . . . This is the common cause of our countries,
> which have joined in the Warsaw Treaty to ensure the inde-
> pendence, the peace and security in Europe. . . . We shall
> never agree to have imperialism, using ways peaceful and non-

peaceful, making a gap from the inside or from the outside in the Socialist system and changing in imperialism's favor the correlation of forces in Europe.[17]

Another major risk in allowing the unimpeded expansion of internal autonomy is that it might create the conditions that would allow the generation of pressures for greater independence from Moscow in foreign policy. These risks and hazards, of course, vary from one country to another, depending largely upon its strategic importance to Soviet security, economic significance, natural resources and its impact and influence upon the other communist countries as a possible model to emulate. While the Soviet leaders might tolerate varying degrees of independence in foreign policy, just as they might allow differentials in internal autonomy, the latitude in foreign policy is less than that in internal affairs because foreign policy strikes more directly at the Soviet power position in world affairs and more vitally affects its security. While the traditionally favorable image that the Czechs held of Russia combined with their fear of German "revanchism" and the Czech penchant for prudence and caution might have been sufficient to allay Soviet qualms that an independent foreign policy would erode Prague's commitments to the Soviet Union and the Warsaw Pact, other developments raised apprehensions in Moscow, frightened Gomulka and appeared downright ominous to Ulbricht. These included not only a possible political and diplomatic rapprochement with West Germany (encouraged by Bonn's repudiation of the Munich agreement of 1938), but also the prospect of a large hard-currency loan from West Germany that might set the stage for a radical reorientation of Czechoslovakia's trade from the Soviet Union and Eastern Europe to Western countries.[18] The fact that such a rearrangement of trade relations coincided with Czech economic interests and was indispensable for economic recovery served to reinforce the fear that a change in trade relations would soon be followed by significant alterations in Prague's political and ideological alignments.

Furthermore, when Brezhnev's mission to save Novotny

failed in December 1967 and particularly after Novotny's suspension from the Party and the discrediting of the secret police by the Dubcek regime, opinion on foreign policy became bolder and, from the Soviet point of view, outrageous. The Jan Masaryk affair was reopened and Moscow's complicity through Mikoyan was alleged, past Soviet interference in Czech affairs was roundly condemned, and demands for a new and more thorough investigation were made in the press. A prominent Czech general challenged Soviet domination of the Warsaw Pact command structure,[19] others called for a reexamination of Prague's role in the Warsaw Pact Organization, while still others demanded that future Czech foreign policy be based on Czech national interests and not on the interests of Moscow, other Communist states, or the world Communist movement.[20] Some even called for a frankly "neutralist" foreign policy.

The Soviet leaders might have adjusted to a wide degree of Czech autonomy in domestic and foreign affairs if they felt that the greater freedom would be restricted only to Czechoslovakia. The decisive factor in a sharply divided Soviet leadership may well have been the real fear that Ulbricht would not be able to resist the pressures for liberalization in East Germany that would inevitably be generated if Dubcek was successful in gaining liberalization in Czechoslovakian affairs. Greater internal autonomy in East Germany would inevitably result in further popular pressures for an independent reexamination of East Germany's role as a separate state bound in permanent vassalage to Russia. Under these conditions Moscow would be confronted with a crisis of incalculable magnitude. The situation might spin out of control and result in a reunited Germany that would fundamentally alter the entire balance of power in Europe and conjure up the nightmare of another German march to the East. At best, an autonomous East Germany would sap Soviet energies and power.

One might even make out a case that the desperate and hasty disavowal of the Bratislava agreement was actually triggered not so much by Dubcek's refusal or inability to satisfy some reputed secret commitment to arrest liberalization but rather by Ulbricht's unexpected gesture of reconciliation with West Germany made soon after his disagreeable meeting with Dubcek and just a few days before the forces of the Warsaw alliance moved across Czech frontiers.[21] To Moscow this may have been an evil omen of impending catastrophe unless she intervened to stop the falling Czech domino.

CZECHOSLOVAKIA, HUNGARY, RUMANIA

The Soviet intervention in Czechoslovakia has been widely compared to the Soviet crackdown in Hungary twelve years earlier and contrasted to Soviet restraint in the face of Rumanian defiance. What accounts for the differences and similiarities in Soviet behavior in the three cases? The Soviet intervention in Hungary was inspired by fears that were both genuine and credible, brought about by provocations that transcended any indulged in by Czechoslovakia. A national anti-Soviet uprising swept Hungary, during which the Imre Nagy regime virtually disestablished the Communist system: the secret police was dismantled and many of its members executed, the multiparty system was restored as the Communist Party disintegrated; political prisoners were released, including Cardinal Mindszenty; Nagy announced Hungary's unilateral withdrawal from the Warsaw Pact and enunciated a "neutralist" foreign policy. It should also be remembered that the Hungarian uprising took place against the background of the Eisenhower-Dulles policy of "liberation," which was avowedly dedicated—in words at least—to the emancipation of the satellites from Soviet domination. Appeals and encouragement of Radio Free Europe appeared to the Kremlin as a further indication of U.S. malevolence and mischief.

In contrast, neither Czechoslovakia nor Rumania threatened to *withdraw* from the Warsaw Pact; neither have threatened to disestablish the Communist social order; neither threatened to pursue a "neutralist" foreign policy. The Communist party has never been threatened with disintegration in either country. Most importantly, developments in Czechoslovakia were proceeding in an atmosphere of détente with a

total absence of any provocations from the United States,
verbal or otherwise.[22]

Yet, while Rumania's isolated geographical location rendered her vulnerable to Soviet pressure, it simultaneously
rendered her defiance of the Soviet Union a minimal threat to
Soviet power and security interests, and the Soviets have
therefore felt less need to interfere. Furthermore, Rumania's
independent policy posed little danger that any other satellite
might also become a problem to Russia. Rumania's defection
did not pose a real threat to Russia or any other Eastern
European country since she was surrounded entirely by Communist states (if one includes Yugoslavia).

On the other hand, Czechoslovakia's geographical location was of signal strategic and security importance not only
to Russia but to Poland and East Germany as well. An independent Czech foreign policy could seriously interfere with
coordinated bloc military or diplomatic action, particularly
where West Germany is concerned. Geographically, Czechoslovakia slices eastern Europe into a "northern tier" (East
Germany and Poland) and a "southern tier" (Hungary, Rumania, Bulgaria, Albania and Yugoslavia). Significantly, the
countries to the north of Prague supported and indeed encouraged Moscow to intervene. while the southern tier with the
exception of Moscow's loyal satrapy of Bulgaria, *i.e.* Hungary,
Rumania, Yugoslavia, and even Albania supported the Dubcek
regime. Hungary reluctantly participated in the military
intervention because it was under Soviet military occupation
itself,[24] but East Germany and Poland participated in the
occupation with considerable enthusiasm.

Not only does Czechoslovakia cut the Eastern European
countries into two parts geographically, but it also conjures
up the image of an "invasion funnel" leading from West Germany to Russia, or a "knife" aimed by West Germany at the
heart of the Ukraine. Decisions, unfortunately, are often influenced by such banal metaphors, as they are by chichés like
Bismark's, "The master of Bohemia is the master of Europe."
In short, one might say that while the risk of a Czech defection from the Soviet Bloc in foreign policy was lower than

that of Rumania, the danger of such a defection would be infinitely greater than a Rumanian defection.

CONCLUSIONS

To intervene or not to intervene: either course would have produced unpalatable and distasteful consequences. Down to virtually the moment of occupation, it appeared that the Soviet Presidium, after its meetings with the Czech leadership at Cierna and Bratislava, had decided, perhaps by a slim margin, that the consequences of nonintervention would be less disagreeable than those of intervention. Unless we succumb to the view that the Soviet leaders engaged in an act of calculated perfidy, it must be assumed that a prior decision was precipitously reversed. This seems to be confirmed by the gross ineptness of the political side of the occupation as contrasted with the quick and smooth efficiency of the military operation. The Soviet action is thus simultaneously a frightening tribute to the immensity of Soviet military power and a dismal monument to its diplomatic ineptitude, political incompetence, grotesque morality, and the utter and complete bankruptcy of Communist ideology. The enormity of the Soviet debacle was permanently enshrined by the pathetic inability of 650,000 Warsaw Pact troops to find the elusive and nameless Czech political leaders who invited them to expel the "Western imperialists," subdue the "counterrevolutionaries," and crush the treacherous "Dubcek clique." [28] Unable to pressure an aged but unyielding President Svoboda to legalize their intervention and unable to persuade even a handful of Czech and Slovak Communists to betray their country by signing the prefabricated Soviet document of invitation and to form a Quisling government, Moscow was forced to deal with the very government which its military forces had arrested. Svoboda was whisked off to Moscow and given a shameless red carpet welcome, while Dubcek, Premier Oldrich Cernik, and National Assembly President Josef Smirkovsky were transported to the Soviet capital to "negotiate" a compromise settlement.

It is an eloquent tribute to Czech courage and perhaps Dubcek's Slovak obstinancy that the Soviet intervention has not been endowed with even a shred of legality and that the faceless sponsors who "invited" the Warsaw powers to occupy their country have not come forward to identify themselves, if indeed they exist at all.

Clearly the Soviet Union has reached an important crossroads in its relationship with Eastern Europe. Before the Czech intervention in Czechoslovakia, the Soviet position in Eastern Europe had clearly been slipping, partly in response to the apparent erosion of NATO and the diminution of the threat of the United States to the Communist system. Either the Soviet empire was on the verge of dissolution—as Rumania virtually seceded from the Warsaw alliance and Czech liberalization appeared to be irresistible and threatened to infect all of Eastern Europe—or it was on the brink of a fundamental transformation.

The transformation of relationships could have assumed one of three forms:

1. The conversion of the Warsaw Pact and CEMA into an authentic socialist "commonwealth of nations," in which the individual members would be allowed a wide latitude of internal deviation from the Soviet norms of socialism, exercise greater freedom in trade and in cultural relations with the West, while remaining tightly bound to the Soviet Union in a purely defensive alliance. Such a transformation would presuppose a continuation and expansion of the détente, a tacit disavowal of ideological aggressiveness in foreign policy, and give greater form and shape to the new commonwealth as a purely regional association, in which the interests of the smaller members would no longer be sacrificed to those of the Soviet Union in the name of the bogus principle of "proletarian internationalism" or subordinated to purely Soviet great power diplomacy in its dealings with the United States or Communist China. The chief objections to such a transformation before August 1968, were that it threatened to isolate East Germany, render Poland even more dependent upon

Russia vis à vis West Germany, and deprive the Soviet Union of some useful levers and pressures in dealing with the German problem, the United States, and Communist China.

2. The natural *devolution* of the Warsaw Pact, CEMA, and other multilateral organizations and their replacement with a series of bilateral and trilateral agreements. The Soviet Union could make periodic *ad hoc* adjustments to the situation, allowing the natural interests of each state more or or less to shape its individual relationship with the Soviet Union. Moscow would rely upon a common ideology, intersecting interests, the prudence and good sense of the smaller countries and the reservoir of goodwill towards Moscow that would flow from such a policy to become the foundations of a new relationship. Under these conditions, the relationship of the individual member states with Russia could vary considerably, as would their relations with one another. The artificiality of imposed "fraternal" relations would be replaced by something more uncertain but perhaps more durable and natural.

3. The reconstitution of the Soviet empire as a "sphere of influence" or domination, similar to the position of the United States in the Caribbean. Wherever and whenever necessary, naked force and fear would be applied rather than the shibboleths of ideology, pliable local leaders, and a common social system, in order to preserve Soviet control.

Apparently Moscow has chosen the third option, which effectively forecloses the other two. It would seem that the Soviet Union by its action in Czechoslovakia has not only expended whatever reservoir of goodwill that remained of the historical, cultural, and ideological associations of the past, but has reduced its options to only two: preserving its position by force, threat, and periodic intervention or allowing its control of Eastern Europe to disintegrate completely. For the moment, the Soviet Union has enhanced the credibility of its determination to use its immense power to control its immediate environment, but simultaneously it has restored its reputation for diplomatic perfidy, impetuous brutality, and psychological insecurity. Not only the Communist world, but the Communist states of Eastern Europe are now irrevocably

split. Although there is no discernible military threat in sight
from any quarter in Europe, the Soviet Union is now in military occupation of no less than four Eastern European countries (Poland, East Germany, Hungary, and Czechoslovakia).
Albania has unilaterally withdrawn from the Warsaw Pact
as a result of the Czech crisis, while Rumania refuses to allow
Warsaw Pact forces to maneuver on its territory and refuses
to participate in their exercises elsewhere. Yugoslavia has
never belonged to the Warsaw Pact and at the height of the
Czech crisis announced its determination, together with Rumania, to resist by armed force any attempt on the part of
Russia to occupy her territories.

The liberalization in Czechoslovakia has been arrested
and is being reversed. Soviet leaders have announced not only
their intention to keep Soviet troops on the Czech-West German frontier indefinitely but are also imposing their dictates
on purely internal Czech affairs. They have refused to allow
Prague to expand its trade relations outside the Soviet bloc.
Like Hungary, Czechoslovakia has been turned from clientage
to vassalage once again. Whereas the initial reaction in the
other countries of Eastern Europe was fear and apprehension
combined with outrage and shame, they are now on notice that
Moscow will not hesitate to reduce its fraternal allies to vassalage if the Soviet Union disapproves of either their internal
or external policies.

What of the future?

As the initial shock wears off and the Czechs continue
their passive resistance and active noncooperation, the people
of Eastern Europe are likely to become more restive than
quiescent. Disturbances might even spread among disaffected
and alienated Soviet intellectuals, scientists, and students.
The moral position of Gomulka has probably been irretriev-
ably damaged, since Gomulka turned against Czechoslovakia
with neither justification nor provocation. Poland, as a consequence, has become more wholely dependent upon the Soviet
Union and is now completely surrounded by countries under
Soviet military occupation, and its people are even more
thoroughly alienated from Moscow. It may be that Gomulka
sold his country's honor to gain a tactical advantage over his

internal rival, General Moczar, and in return for a mess of pottage established a precedent for a future Soviet military occupation of Poland in the guise of "multilateral" action.

The Soviet military occupation of Czechoslovakia ushers Soviet relations with Eastern Europe into a new phase—a phase of Soviet military control. This new phase should not be confused with the earlier Stalinist period. During the Stalin era, Moscow relied not only upon the Soviet military presence, but upon a common ideology and more importantly upon the reliability and servility of the local Communist Party. This is no longer even residually the case in Rumania, Yugoslavia, Albania, or Czechoslovakia (in spite of the occupation). Communist parties in Eastern European countries will continue to pay greater and greater attention to national needs rather than Soviet dictates and interests, although the danger of a desperate Soviet intervention has increased. Interventionism itself, however, is a wasting asset and cannot be sustained indefinitely, and thus the Soviet military occupation of Czechoslovakia simultaneously signifies a Soviet determination to reintensify its control, and risks contracting its range of control.

In spite of the Soviet action, as time goes on the ideological bond of Communism will continue to erode, and Eastern European countries will become more European and less "Communist." Today everywhere in Eastern Europe, in stark contrast to the Soviet Union, Communism appears as a thin, almost transparent, veneer, ready to be shed at the first felicitous moment. Fundamental and far-reaching transformations are still imminent in Eastern Europe, and perhaps for at least another decade, changes will be made in the name of Communism while the system itself is being subverted. Although similar changes will also take place in Russia, the necessity or desire to disavow Communism as an ideology may not be nearly as intense. After all, Soviet society and Marxism-Leninism are Russian creations and thus are not as incompatible with Russian nationalism as they are with the nationalisms of non-Soviet countries. It must be remembered that whereas the Communist system is an indigenous Russian phenomenon, in Eastern Europe it is an alien, imported system imposed from the outside by force. Thus, although Communism and nationalism may be fused into a "Soviet patriotism" in the Soviet Union, this is by no means an assured amalgam in Eastern Europe.

Communism is now irrevocably associated with Russian and/or Soviet imperialism, domination, and control, and although this may have a minimal vitiating effect in countries traditionally pro-Russian, it may simultaneously be a barrier to its complete acceptance, assimilation, and adaptation in the traditionally anti-Russian countries of Eastern Europe. At least another decade will be required before permanent trends are conclusively discernible, when a new generation of leaders and citizens make their appearance in both Russia and Eastern Europe.

NOTES

1. See V. V. Aspaturian, "Dialectics and Duplicity in Soviet Diplomacy," *Journal of International Affairs*, No. 1 (1963), pp. 42–58, and "Diplomacy in the Mirror of Soviet Scholarship," in J. Keep, editor, *Contemporary History in the Soviet Mirror* (New York: Frederick C. Praeger, 1965), pp. 243–74.

2. For a more complete treatment of the author's view of this point, see the following: "Soviet Foreign Policy," in R. C. Macridis, editor, *Foreign Policy in World Politics*, third edition (Englewood Cliffs, N.J.: Prentice-Hall, 1967); "Moscow's Foreign Policy," *Survey* (October, 1967), pp. 35–60; "Internal Politics and Foreign Policy in the Soviet System," in R. B. Farrell, editor, *Approaches to Comparative and International Politics* (Evanston, Ill.: North-

western University Press, 1966), pp. 212–87.

4. For the standard work on the evolution of Soviet relations with Eastern Europe, see Zbigniew Brzezinski, *The Soviet Bloc*, revised and enlarged edition (Cambridge, Mass.: Harvard University Press, 1967). For the author's interpretation of the Soviet role, see V. V. Aspaturian, *The Soviet Union in the World Communist Movement* (Stanford, Calif.: The Hoover Institution, 1966) and the author's "The Soviet Union and International Communism," in R. C. Macridis, *op. cit.*, pp. 216–46.

5. See D. Floyd, *Rumania, Russia's Dissident Ally* (New York: Frederick C. Praeger, 1965), and Ghita Ionescu, *The Break-up of the Soviet Empire in Eastern Europe* (Baltimore: Penguin Books, 1965).

6. See excerpts from Ceausescu's speech in *The New York Times* (March 14, 1966). In this speech the Rumanian leader also condemned past Soviet interference in the affairs of the Rumanian Communist party and Rumanian internal affairs, and expressed resentment at the manner in which Bessarabia was annexed by Moscow.

7. See *Pravda* (March 5, 7, and 9, 1968) and *The New York Times* (March 2, 8, and 9, 1968).

8. East Germany, the only divided national state in eastern Europe, was actually under full Soviet military occupation, while Poland and Hungary were under partial Soviet occupation, and Bulgaria was and remains supinely servile, East Germany's status was improved by the Czech occupation while the autonomy of Poland and Hungary was seriously compromised.

9. For an accounting of the diversity in institutions, policies, and tendencies developing in Eastern Europe, *see* the following: Ghita Ionéscu, *The Politics of the European Communist States* (New York: Frederick C. Praeger, 1967), and H. Gordon Skilling, *The Governments of Communist East Europe* (New York: Crowell, 1966); Kurt London, *Eastern Europe in Transition* (Baltimore: The John Hopkins Press, 1966); and J. Triska, *The World Communist System* (Stanford, Stanford Studies of the Communist System, 1964).

10. See William Griffith, *Albania and the Sino-Soviet Rift* (Cambridge: The M.I.T. Press, 1963).

11. For an analysis of the sources of diversity, see R. V. Burks, *The Dynamics of Commu-*

nism in Eastern Europe (Princeton: Princeton University Press, 1961).

12. See "Is The Situation Norml?" a denunciation of "creeping counterrevolution" in *Izvestia* (July 31, 1968) and A. Butenko, "Under the False Flag of 'Building Bridges,'" *Izvestia* (May 16, 1968), where it is alleged, "first 'bridges' and then a 'revision of the status quo,' that it, a revision of the existing boundaries in Europe." See also M. Volgin, "Bridges on Rotten Foundations," *Izvestia* (July 11, 1968); "The Strategy of Imperialism and the Czechoslovak Socialist Republic," *Pravda* (July 15, 1968); I. Aleksandrov's article in *Pravda* (July 11, 1958). "Attack on the Socialist Foundations of Czechslovakia," in which he ominously compares the "counterrevolutionary" situation in Czechoslovakia with that of Hungary in 1956; V. Bakinsky's "Whom Doctor Henzl is Defending," *Izvestia* (July 13, 1968), which stresses the ultimate consequences of allowing "antisocialist" elements and "counterrevolutionaries" free rein in Czechoslovakia, and finally the *Pravda* editorial of August 22, 1968, justifying the intervention, "Defender of Socialism is the Highest International Duty."

13. For the ventilation of Soviet fears concerning press freedom in Czechoslovakia, see Yuri Zhukov, "Strange Undertaking of *Obrana Lidu*," *Pravda* (July 27, 1968), and "Double Game," *Pravda* (July 28, 1968). For Soviet attacks on Czech "revisions" of recent history, see A. Nedorov, "Contrary to the Facts," *Izvestia* (June 29, 1968), and "What Does 'The Student' Teach?—The Prague Weekly 'for Young Intelligentsia' and Its Concept of Democracy,"

Komsomolskaya Pravda (June 21, 1968). Moscow was particularly incensed at the renewed interest in the Masaryks and attempts to re-write the recent history of Czech-German relations, which it inter-preted to be an intellectual prepa-ration for a rapprochement with Bonn. See also A. Kamshalov. "So-cialism and Young People," *Kom-somolskaya Pravda* (July 20, 1968) and the attacks upon Jan Prochazka in *Literaturnaya Ga-zeta* (May 19 and June 26, 1968).

14. This was reflected in the vicious Soviet attacks upon the political manifesto, "2000 Words," which called upon the Dubcek re-gime to purge the party of No-votny followers, and contained a savage criticism of the party as the source of Prague's ills for the past twenty years. See the abridg-ed text in *Washington Post* (July 21, 1968) and for Soviet attacks, see *Pravda* (July 11, 1968), the attack upon Frantisek Kriegel in *Literaturnaya Gazeta* (July 10, 1968), the attack upon Josef Bo-ruvka, a member of the Czech Presidium, for approving the no-tion of a non-Communist opposition in *Pravda* (March 9, 1968), and N. Vladimirov's attacks on the new "political clubs" in Czechoslo-vakia, "The 'Political Instincts' of Vaclav Havel," *Literaturnaya Ga-zeta* (May 15, 1968).

15. This was the crux of the warnings in the Dresden and War-saw statements and a major reason for the necessity of intervention in *Pravda* (August 22, 1968).

16. See *Pravda* (March 25, 1968), for text of communique, and for a Soviet commentary, see I. Aleksandrov. "Slanderer's Fabrica-tions are Doomed to Failure," *Pravda* (March 28, 1968).

17. Full text in *Pravda* (July 18, 1968).

18. Moscow feared that not only Prague but other Eastern Eu-ropean states might be attracted by the blandishments of West Ger-many's "new eastern Policy," which became a focus of Soviet attack. See Gromyko's speech to the Supreme Soviet, *Pravda* (June 28, 1968); "What They Hope for in Bonn," *Izvestia* (May 15, 1968); "Secret Arms Caches at the Bor-der with the F.R.G.," *Pravda* (July 19, 1968); "F.R.G. Interference in Czechoslovak Affairs," *Pravda* (July 20, 1968); V. Mikhailov, "In the Revanchists' Sights," *Pravda* (July 22, 1968); L. Kamyin, "Re-vanchists' Orgy," *Izvestia* (July 26, 1968); V. Zhigulenko, "To the Beat of Drums," *Izvestia* (July 27, 1968); and Y. Grigoryev, "A Hoof Wrapped in Rags," *Pravda* (July 28, 1968). Professor Zbigniew Brzezinski, a former member of the State Department's Policy Planning Staff, came in for con-siderable condemnation as the ide-ologist of the "building bridges" policy and the architect of the plan to "isolate" East Germany. See Brzezinski's *Alternative to Partition* (New York: McGraw-Hill, 1965); Willy Brandt, "Ger-man Policy Toward the East," *Foreign Affairs* (April, 1968); Adam Bronke and P. E. Uren, *The Communist States and The West* (New York: Frederick C. Praeger, 1967), and *The Atlantic Commu-nity and Eastern Europe* (The Atlantic Institute, 1967).

19. General Vaclav Prchlik, head of the Military Department of the Central Committee of the Czech Communist party. See *The New York Times* (July 16 and 19, 1968). For the Soviet reaction, see the *Krasnaya Zvezda* editorial, "Whose Favor is General V. Prch-lik Currying?" (July 23, 1968), prompting Prague to reassign the

General, which failed to satisfy Moscow.

20. In particular, the views of Jan Prochazka, who advocated a restricted role in international affairs for Czechoslovakia, based upon her own needs and interests: "We are a small country. . . . We should have a modest foreign policy, one conforming to our possibilities. I do not understand why we have to intervene in the affairs of Madagascar, Guatemala or Nigeria." See "The Train Jan Prochazka Missed," *Literaturnaya Gazeta* (May 19, 1968), and N. Vladimirov, "On Which Roof is Jan Prochazka Sitting?" *Literaturnaya Gazeta* (June 26, 1968); see also Moscow's attack on "The Student," *Komsomolskaya Pravda* (June 21, 1968).

21. See *The New York Times* (August 18, 1968).

22. This did not prevent Moscow from indulging in fantasies and fabrications concerning the role of the U.S. See V. Ragulin and I. Chushkov, "Adventurist Plans of the Pentagon and the C.I.A." *Pravda* (July 19, 1968); B. Strelnikov, "Trojan Horse of American Propaganda," *Pravda* (July 29, 1968); Yuri Zhukov, "Instigators," *Pravda* (August 16, 1968); and N. Matveyev, "Poisoned Pens," *Izvestia* (August 17, 1968). Rusk's tepid protest at this gratuitous involvement was routinely shrugged off by Ambassador Dobrynin and the Soviet Foreign Ministry.

23. Ceausescu charged in May, 1966, that Moscow deliberately staffed the Rumanian Communist party with nonethnic Rumanians and emigrés to keep it in a permanent condition of servility. *The New York Times* (May 14, 1966).

24. One prominent Hungarian, the chief editor of *Nepszabadzag*,

for example, rejected in a speech before the Hungarian Parliament the Moscow charge that the situation in Czechoslovakia was similar to that of Hungary in 1956. *The New York Times* (July 14, 1968).

25. C. Cisar, a secretary of the Czech Central Committee, in *Rude Pravo* (May 7, 1968). Cisar later attempted to soften his position, but he was severely attacked by the prominent Soviet ideologist F. Konstantinov in *Pravda* on June 14, 1968, "Marxism-Leninism is a Unified International Doctrine," and on July 24, 1968, "Leninism is the Marxism of the Present Era." See also I. Pomelov, "Common Principles and National Characteristics in the Development of Socialism," *Pravda* (August 14, 1968), which concentrated its fire on national variations of "socialism" and "Communism."

26. See, for example, the remarkable document on "convergence" by the Soviet scientist Andrei D. Sakharov, who called upon the Soviet leaders to support and praise Czech liberalization. Full text in *The New York Times* (July 22, 1968).

27. See the Sakharov statement, cited above.

28. The "invitation" was necessary to provide the bare minimum basis of legality for the intervention, for the Warsaw Treaty does not give the member states the blanket authority, collectively or individually, to unilaterally declare the existence of "counterrevolutionaries" and/or external "imperialist forces" and intervene on their own initiative. The juridical scenario employed by Moscow was virtually a carbon copy of the intervention of the United States and the OAS in the Dominican Republic. The so-called "invitation," published by *Pravda* and *Izvestia*

on August 21, 1968, justified the
intervention on both internal and
external grounds:

> Tass is authorized to state
> that party and state leaders of
> the Czechoslovak Socialist Re-
> public requested the Soviet
> Union and other allied states
> to give the fraternal Czecho-
> slovak people immediate as-
> sistance, including assistance
> with armed forces. The reason
> for this appeal is the threat
> posed to the socialist system
> existing in Czechoslovakia and
> to the constitutionally estab-
> lished state system by counter-
> revolutionary forces that have
> entered into collusion with
> external forces hostile to
> socialism.

U.S. Policy and the
Invasion of Czechoslovakia

by William E. Griffith

The recent policy of the United States towards Czechoslovakia has been, in my view, short-sighted and shameful. In
order to explain briefly why, in my opinion, it deserves to be
characterized by such strong adjectives, I must begin by out-
lining my own analytical assumptions. What were the causes
for the developments in Czechoslovakia between 1967 and
1968? What were their implications for Russia and the United
States?

Czechoslovakia was liberalized between 1962 and 1968
by the interaction of five factors.[1] The first was destalinization,
as a result of which Novotny's prestige was destroyed by
making public his complicity in crime. The second was the
serious economic recession that took place in 1962 caused by
the increasingly inefficient, centralized, Stalinist economic
model: low worker productivity, disruption in foreign trade
patterns, extensive Soviet-directed aid to the third world, and
low agricultural output. This recession convinced the Czech
and Slovak intelligentsia that drastic economic reforms, the
end of wage egalitarianism, and a massive infusion of high-
level Western technology were necessary in order to make
Czechoslovak exports internationally competitive once again,

and that, because Novotny would not agree to these reforms, which would threaten his political power, he must go. The third was the recoalescence and return to power of the Czech and Slovak intelligentsia, who upheld the leftist, social democratic traditions of Masaryk and the First Republic, as well as moderate traditions of Czechoslovak Communism, as they existed before 1929. The fourth was the development by the Czech intelligentsia of a more favorable attitude toward the West Germans and of a less favorable one to the East Germans and the Russians, for the intelligentsia began to realize that the Soviet Union was technologically inferior to the West, and that, however politically undesirable, there was no other source for both Western technology and investment credits than West Germany, which was largely democratized. They also began to resent Ulbricht's and Moscow's support of Novotny and rigid Soviet control over Czechoslovakia. The fifth factor, the Slovak nationalist revolt and demand for autonomy and equality, was the immediate cause of Novotny's fall.

In order to dispose of Novotny, Dubcek removed the controls that had existed over the communications media. Thereupon, journalists and intellectuals called for economic rationalization, free speech and press, equality for the Slovaks, improvement of political and economic relations with the West (including the United States, and inevitably, because of the need for technology and credits, with West Germany), plus a degree of political opposition which, many hoped and expected, would lead to a genuine multiparty system.

Dubcek only partially controlled and limited the reform wave and became himself more liberal in the process. Yet he was determined to rehabilitate Communism through reform, not to replace it by democratic socialism. He also was determined to maintain what he saw as the three essentials of Communism in Czechoslovakia: alliance with Moscow, continuing nationalization of industry, and a Communist Party federalized but continuing to control society; other interest groups would be consulted but would not be allowed to form opposition parties.

For a comparatively long time the Soviet leadership was divided and hesitant about invading Czechoslovakia—longer than Tsar Nicholas I would have been! They finally invaded because they feared that Dubcek would not or could not protect the essentials of Communism; that the KSC party conservatives would be purged; that opposition parties and press freedom would be established and would bring rising criticism of East Germany, Poland, and Russia itself; that the Ukraine would thereby be infected (notably via liberalization and Slovak federalization) ; that, in order to modernize and make his economy competitive, Dubcek would even though unwillingly accept more West German credits than the $375 million granted to Rumania and that thereby West Germany would begin to replace Soviet economic and then political influence in Czechoslovakia; and that, consequently, East Germany would be destabilized and isolated.

In sum, the leaders of the Soviet Union realized (correctly, in my view) that they could not continue their present form of imperial rule in eastern Europe, and even in the long run its present repression in the USSR unless they crushed the Czechoslovak liberalization.

Thus, the invasion was primarily an assertion of Great Russian imperialism, not "proletarian internationalism." Indeed, the Thermidor of Bolshevism may well become a peaceful transition into Great Russian Fascism: imperialism, anti-intellectualism, anti-Semitism, anti-Westernism. In the short run, since they seem determined to move toward more extremism in general at home and abroad, the Soviet leaders thus probably had no alternative policy. In the long run, however, their prospects in Eastern Europe seem to me to be less favorable. The invasion will not only not solve but will probably make it more difficult for Moscow to solve Soviet and East European technological backwardness and to contain indefinitely East European nationalism.

The Soviets restored their domination in Czechoslovakia. They also stifled any tendencies in Hungary, Poland, East Germany, or Bulgaria toward liberalization or independence, and checked a major potential success for West Germany. Moscow, however, also greatly worsened its relations with Yugoslavia, Rumania (although the latter has much less room for maneuver) and West European Communist parties, who for the first time almost unanimously denounced the Soviet invasion, as have the Chinese and the New Left. Castro, dependent on Soviet aid, endorsed Moscow but only in order to try to push Soviet policy in a more militant, anti-American direction, and for the first time publicly asked for a Soviet military guarantee. The disintegration of NATO and unilateral withdrawal of United States troops from West Germany was at least delayed. West Germany, more fearful of Moscow, remained less likely to move away from the United States. West Germany suspended its decision to begin ministerial-level discussions with East Berlin, which Russia and East Germany did prefer. Franco-American relations improved as a result of the French assessment of the invasion and the increasing Soviet naval presence in the Mediterranean and influence in Algeria. The loss of international prestige and influence that the United States suffered from its Vietnam policy was at least in part offset by the loss Russia suffered from the world-wide outcry against Moscow's occupation of Czechoslovakia. Finally, the blow to East-West détente slowed down U.S. and—more importantly for Moscow—West German ratification of the nonproliferation treaty, as well as the initiation of strategic weapons negotiations between the United States and Russia.

In short, by restoring their control over Czechoslovakia, the Russians blocked any potential deviations in Poland, East Germany, Hungary, and Bulgaria, but in the rest of the world their influence suffered. Even in Czechoslovakia, where the Good Soldier Svejk's tradition of silent, concealed, but persistent opposition to foreign domination is long, Dubcek, Svoboda, and the Czech and Slovak peoples will hardly soon forgive or forget. The Soviet invasion probably ended the long tradition of pro-Russian feeling among the Czechs, who will now bide their time and husband their strength for the long, complex struggle ahead.

After the invasion, the immediate options were clearer than the final choices. The Soviets could try to turn Dubcek into an unwilling instrument to support their foreign policy, notably against West Germany, and make him purge his liberal colleagues, repress domestic dissent, lose his popular support, and thus be able to survive only through Soviet backing—or they could remove him and try the same with his successor. As long as Dubcek remains in office, he and his associates will try to be only as repressive as they feel compelled to be and to maintain an unspoken national conspiracy of *attentisme,* holding out for better days. Limited economic decentralization, as in East Germany, will be allowed as long as political repression continues, and Slovak autonomy, although discouraged, will be permitted as long as it does not further liberalization or weaken Soviet control. The Russians anticipate that the shock of the invasion will soon be overshadowed in the West by its desire to resume an East-West détente, as happened after the invasion of Hungary.

Has the Soviet invasion of Czechoslovakia decisively and permanently reversed the trend toward autonomy and liberalization in Eastern Europe or will the indigenous forces for national communism again revive? On balance, it seems to me unlikely that any permanent reversal has occurred. Rather, the invasion has probably only limited and slowed down tendencies that will reoccur.

This appears likely for reasons arising out of Soviet as well as East European affairs. As to the former, I share Zbigniew Brezezinski's view that Soviet society is tending toward bureaucratic rigidity [2] and that the countervailing forces of intellectual ferment, tensions among nationalities, and economic revisionism make a full-scale reversion to Stalinist imperialism in Eastern Europe extremely difficult. Brezhnev has neither Stalin's complete power nor the former dictator's iron conviction that his own solutions should be imposed regardless of cost in life or rubles. Nor did Khrushchev. And the likelihood that even a new and more charismatic leader in Moscow could reconsolidate the Soviet political elite without the aid of wartime pressure is slim.

As to Eastern Europe, modernization increases popular pressures on their regimes for reform, which may be controlled as it is in East Germany or get out of hand as it did in Czechoslovakia and Yugoslavia. If politicization outruns institutionalization it leads to political decay (e.g. Poland). Everywhere politicization and nationalism, combined with the demand for economic growth, threaten rigidly centralized regimes. Moreover, the attraction of Western Europe, and particularly the economic pull of West Germany, can be temporarily contained but hardly obliterated. Thus an interim period of repression and then a period of a slower, more limited resumption of liberalization seem to me the most likely prospect for Eastern Europe.

I now turn to a reassessment of Soviet policies in the light of the invasion. First, the present Soviet leadership has within the last few years adopted a more oppressive policy at home and a more expansionist one abroad, and refuses to loosen its grip on the northern East European states. Russia therefore will apparently intervene in what it considers a strategically vital East European country even if the latter does not intend to break with Moscow and remains under control of its Communist Party. When the Russian leaders become convinced that there exists a clear threat to Soviet hegemony or a rise in West German influence they will intervene. They are even more likely to do so if the country had become politically more liberal and Communist Party control has declined to such an extent that the liberalization might spread to East Germany, Poland, and Russia itself. Any change in the politics of Eastern Europe therefore depends, as it has since 1945, upon changes in Soviet policy itself, which has not as yet occurred and seems unlikely to do so in the near future. Second, the invasion showed Moscow's readiness to use rapid, overwhelming force in Eastern Europe with little or no reliable advance warning to the West. Third, the invasion of Czechoslovakia also indicated that the influence of East Germany and Poland on deterring liberalization is greater than had been previously assumed. Fourth, it demonstrated major Soviet concern over the spread in Eastern Europe of West German economic and technological influence. Finally, it revealed disunity and indecisiveness within the Soviet leadership that may reoccur in other areas of Soviet policy.

The primary implications of the Soviet invasion of Czechoslovakia relate to American policy toward the Soviet Union —and not to policy toward Eastern Europe. The inadequate information about Russian policy, its hesitation and reversals, and its heightened willingness to use force, all require a general reassessment of willingness to take, in both the strategic and conventional fields. In theory, deterrence is based on reliable calculations of the opponent's intentions (his "rationality"). Logically, the Soviet invasion of Czechoslovakia requires that the United States raise its estimate of Soviet willingness to risk war to achieve its goals. Consequently, the American posture of deterrence should be strengthened in order to achieve higher credibility. Such a rise in US deterrent credibility is in fact under way by MIRV and "thin" ABM deployment.

In Europe the military situation has changed significantly. For the first time in modern history Russian divisions are stationed on the Czechoslovak-Bavarian border. Although this does not increase the size of the Warsaw Pact forces, it advances their forward deployment in an area confronting American ground forces. This makes significant unilateral withdrawals of American forces from central Europe undesirable and unlikely in the near future. It also makes undesirable any further decrease in British, French, or West German forces as well. Finally, the rapidity, massiveness, and professional competence of the Soviet invasion require an urgent reassessment of the NATO early warning system.

The policy of peaceful engagement begun by President Truman was a logical consequence of the economic and military aid granted to Yugoslavia by the United States, which enabled Belgrade to consolidate its independent course. Pursued by Truman's successors, it was a policy of the possible, an attempt to act, even if slowly and in a limited fashion, rather than merely verbally to condemn. The post-Stalin Soviet policy of peaceful coexistence, including active engagement in East and West Europe, was its counterpart. Peaceful engagement, however, was not directed toward removing all Soviet influence from Eastern Europe and did not intend to substitute Western penetration for Russian control. Rather, its purpose was to heal peacefully the division of Europe into East and West "with the consent of the East European countries and the Soviet Union." Peaceful change in

Eastern Europe became possible in part because of such Western acts of "measured firmness" as the Berlin airlift.[3] Peaceful engagement thus presupposes adequate deterrent strength, coupled with willingness for reciprocal lowering of tensions through such measures as mutual, inspected troop withdrawals. It relies upon trade and cultural exchange as incentives to Eastern European states to transform themselves into political organisms less totally dependent upon Russia (but not hostile to it) and with more open domestic policies.

Without the support of the United States for peaceful engagement and détente, developments such as the recent Czechoslovak liberalization would have been hindered, and similar developments in the future would be less likely. Conversely, Russia might not have crushed it had the United States been more restrained in its relations with Moscow while the Soviets were deciding whether to invade.

The basic policy of peaceful engagement in my view remains valid. It was, however, always intended to be used with discrimination. Yugoslavia's and Rumania's condemnation of the invasion should thus be viewed positively, but the Soviet move, and Polish, Hungarian, Bulgarian, and East German participation in it, should be viewed negatively.

These criteria imply the intensification of trade and cultural exchange with Yugoslavia and Rumania—specifically, most-favored-nation treatment for Rumania and authorization of dollar credits for US wheat purchases and dinar credits for US investment in Yugoslavia, plus the withdrawal of most-favored-nation treatment from Poland and the refusal to grant it to Hungary or Bulgaria. Should Yugoslavia so desire, we should assist it to maintain a firm deterrent posture against any Soviet military threat.

Thus, cultural exchange with all the countries that invaded Czechoslovakia, and first of all with Russia, should be temporarily cut back. The Soviet-American flight agreement should also be suspended. The suspensions should be continued until it is clear that Soviet policy in Czechoslovakia will not harden further but, rather, allow some of the reforms to be effected.

Our reassessment of policy toward Moscow should also be

brought into accord with our reassessment of our policy toward Peking. What Doak Barnett has proposed as "containment without isolation" of Communist China is similar to peaceful engagement toward it: a policy of the possible, of preparing for the day after Mao, by putting ourselves in a less hostile posture toward Peking and thus furthering moderation there. There is another, more immediately compelling reason, in my view, for revising now our policy toward Communist China: why, after the invasion, should we continue to not only relieve Moscow of its great fear, a US-Chinese coalition, but also, in effect, join them in total hostility toward Peking? Our conflict of interest with China is less than the Soviet Union's: Moscow holds vast territories in Siberia and Central Asia which the Tsars took from the Manchu Emperors, and the shared Marxist-Leninist ideology exacerbates, not improves, the Sino-Soviet split. Let us, therefore, realize that we shall continue to be in a fundamentally competitive situation with both Moscow and Peking, and therefore adjust our posture toward both so that we may contribute toward their remaining as competitive to each other as to us; thus we will have room for maneuver between them. After all, as Lord Salisbury wisely remarked: "Her Majesty's Government has neither permanent friends nor permanent enemies but only permanent interests." [4]

I now return to my initial statement that the policy of the United States towards the invasion of Czechoslovakia—or more accurately the lack thereof—was short-sighted and shameful. It was in my opinion short-sighted because President Johnson did not foresee that if the Soviets invaded Czechoslovakia he would be compelled to acquiesce to a postponement of the ratification of the nonproliferation treaty and of the start of strategic weapons discussions with Russia. When, in the spring of 1968, some of us proposed that the Soviets should be specifically informed that the signing of the treaty and the talks would (unfortunately) be delayed if they invaded, others argued that because the treaty and the strategic weapons negotiations were more in our interest than in the Soviets' we should not use this threat. This assessment was mistaken, in my view, for two reasons. First, the signing of the

treaty and the start of the weapons discussions are more in
the interest of Russia than of the United States. Moscow wants
the treaty in order to prevent West Germany from gaining
access to nuclear weapons, for this is a greater potential danger to them than our more general—and valid—fears of proliferation are to us. The Soviets would like the weapons
discussions to freeze the near-parity they have obtained in
land-based missiles. In any case, Washington should have
known that an invasion would force us to postpone the treaty
and weapons discussions. Therefore we had nothing to lose
by telling the Soviets, and perhaps it might have helped to
deter them. To the counter-argument that we did not know
if this would work, my answer remains that we could not
know and indeed never can be sure of any policy's effect, but
that is no reason to give up the policy.

Our inaction also was shameful, in my view, for two
reasons. First, the United States was unwilling to risk any of
what it saw as its interests to help preserve from invasion a
country that it had helped found and whose liberalization it
had favored. Second, the inaction of the United States, I
suspect, reflected in part the desire of President Johnson for
a summit meeting with Kosygin to begin the weapons discussions. In view of the then-forthcoming presidential elections,
we might most charitably assume that he wanted to gain political profit therefrom. A more charitable interpretation
would be that personal vanity also played a role.

What should the United States do? First, it should make
plans to deal with increased Soviet pressure on Czechoslovakia,
involving something like the removal of Svoboda, Dubcek, and
others. Such a plan in my view should involve informing the
Soviets that this would mean the end of the Nuclear Proliferation Treaty, for the West Germans and for us, and the end
of the strategic weapons negotiations. We should continue our
cuts in cultural exchange to the invading countries, intensify
exchanges with East European countries who did not invade,
and pursue, in general, those policies suggested above which
have not been implemented. We should ratify the nonproliferation treaty only if the Soviets indicate to us that the situation
in Prague will not sharply deteriorate, if only to avoid the

"Versailles syndrome." Although we should continue to encourage western Europe, Japan, India, Israel, and others to ratify the treaty, we should not do so to the extent that it is as detrimental to other American interests in these areas as it has been to date. We should open the strategic weapons discussions while making publicly clear that we intend to maintain qualitative strategic and conventional superiority over the Soviet Union.

Some may say, with considerable truth, that the Soviet invasion of Czechoslovakia was not so unfavorable to the interests of the United States—it reconsolidated NATO. However, the continuation of the Czechoslovak experiment would have been in my view even more advantageous for all concerned, including the United States. Now, as before the invasion, our enlightened self-interest, a "decent respect for the opinions of mankind," and our realization that Czechoslovakia—even if, as Chamberlain put it, "a far-away country of which we know little" has some moral call on our conscience should convince us that more can and should be done by Washington to try to influence Moscow to loosen its oppressive grasp on that tragic country.

NOTES

1. See, for more extensive analysis and bibliographies, William E. Griffith, "Eastern Europe after the Soviet Invasion of Czechoslovakia," RAND P-3983, October 9, 1968.

2. Zbigniew Brzezinski, "The Soviet Political System: Transformation or Degeneration?" *Problems of Communism*, XV, No. 1 (January–February, 1966), 1–15.

3. Speech by President Johnson, October 7, 1966, *Department of State Bulletin*, October 24, 1966, pp. 622–25. See Zbigniew Brzezinski and William E. Griffith, "Peaceful Engagement in Eastern Europe," *Foreign Affairs* (July, 1961).

4. See Zbigniew Brzezinski, "Meeting Moscow's 'Limited Coexistence,'" *The New Leader*, LI, No. 24 (December 16, 1968), 11–13.

NATO After Czechoslovakia

by Andrew Pierre

Political scientists writing on policy issues must always keep one eye on the calendar. Asked to be predictive three months after the Soviet intervention in Czechoslovakia I wrote in the introduction to this chapter: "Speculations concerning the future are of necessity based to some extent on our knowledge and understanding of the past. Therefore making such speculations is uncommonly difficult when it is occurrences in the extremely recent past which must guide our thinking. For we know only too well that events acquire a different coloration when seen from the perspective of time. The Soviet intervention in Czechoslovakia will be no exception; this may be the case to a remarkable degree for we have no way of knowing now whether the event will be a silent milestone in the history of this decade or merely one minor step in a cascading series of events."

At this writing a year has passed. Pompidou has replaced de Gaulle. The Social Democrats have come into full power in West Germany, and the Nixon Administration has had the opportunity to reshape American policy. How have the predictions of the future, made in the past, withstood the passage of time? The reader will have the opportunity to judge for himself as he reads the chapter as it was written a year ago. Subsequently in the closing pages I examine events of the past

59

year from two differing perspectives—the role of historical
accident upon events and the role of broader, more predictable
historical forces.

*   *   *

The five-power invasion of Czechoslovakia on August 21
blighted overnight the policies of détente pursued by the Western nations in their dealings with the Soviet orbit. In recent
years France, the Federal Republic of Germany and the
United States, in particular, have adopted policies toward
Eastern Europe which were designed to encourage the liberalization of the Communist regimes and wean them away from
their close associations with the Soviet Union. We have now
been reminded that bridge building requires strong pillars at
both ends and that the Eastern pillar of the satellite nations
may collapse if it is undercut at the Soviet base. The individual
Eastern policies of the three above-mentioned nations, although based on certain commonly perceived purposes in
détente, have not been fashioned in one mold. Rather, they
have reflected differing national interests and perspectives and
have been pursued independently of each other. Consequently,
the moods of frustration and anger being felt in Paris, Bonn,
and Washington are of varying hues and orders of magnitude.

Most interesting is the case of France. The damage to
Gaullist hopes and foreign policy has been severe. When de
Gaulle traveled to Warsaw in September, 1967, to speak before
the Polish Sejm and called for "détente, entente and cooperation," he was giving expression to a traditional interest, most
manifest in the 1920s, of a French "presence" in Eastern
Europe. The recently revived French enthusiasm for wide
contacts with the nations of Eastern Europe has been based,
however, on far more than the cultural congeniality and the
search for prestige (although it is true that the French have
often felt loved in Eastern Europe, where they have represented the essence of Western civilization). Rather, de Gaulle's
vision of the Europe of the future, extending "from the At-

lantic to the Urals," has required a considerable loosening of the main political blocs. Without a series of independent states east of Germany—which would serve both to expand Europe to the point where it could balance the United States and the Soviet Union, and to contain Germany—"l'Europe des Patries" would of necessity remain a mirage. The erosion of support for NATO, the criticism of American domination of Western Europe, and the insistence upon the ability of the European nations to take care of their own concerns was dependent upon the willingness of Moscow to act reasonably.

Understandably, then, de Gaulle is reported to have been particularly embittered by the Soviet intervention. Moscow had thrown a sickle in his plans and it is likely that significant new French initiatives in Eastern Europe have been precluded for some time. Public confidence in his Eastern policy had been shaken and the Paris-invoked image of a Soviet Union desirous of "cooperating" with France had been tarnished. The General skillfully deflected domestic criticism of his policies by his use of the Yalta Conference as a lightening rod. Although he condemned the Soviet invasion, he noted that the 1945 Yalta Agreement had divided Europe into two blocs and had established the hegemony of the strongest power in each grouping, thus permitting by tacit agreement their domination over the continent.

In time the Gaullist regime will undoubtedly return to the quest for a Europe for the Europeans, preferably as a *Pax Franca* led by France. The devolution of the Eastern bloc into fully sovereign states is seen as inevitable, since no ideology, even Communism, will prevail over national sentiments and human liberty. France will therefore once again work for détente between the states of Western and Eastern Europe and the formation of a European equilibrium. Paris will have less interest in a détente between the United States and the Soviet Union since their confrontation is useful to the extent that it increases its own room for maneuver. On the other hand, there is likely to be little talk of a possible "reversal of alliances" through which France might move closer to the Soviet Union in order to balance the American dominance in Western Europe. Already French cooperation with the integrated com-

mand of NATO has increased and the previous criticism of
Washington has been restrained. In time, because of domestic,
social and economic disequilibriums, and a new perception of
Germany, the Gaullist regime may also relax its opposition to
British entry into the Common Market.

In West Germany, as in France, the Russian tanks which
rumbled into Prague also crushed a good many hopes for a
European détente. There is a tragic echo in Bonn to the Soviet
action for it totally upset the constructive Eastern policy of the
Kiesinger-Brandt government and probably seriously aggra-
vated the German "problem." Suddenly, now, the Germans
have found themselves back in the cold.

Upon coming into office twenty months earlier the new
"Grand Coalition" took one step further toward the delicate
task of creating an opening to the East. The Hallstein doctrine
was fully discarded, and through expanded trade relations, increased cultural and tourist contacts, and closer and more
active governmental intercourse, the Bonn government not
without difficulty attempted to foster a climate of mutual trust
with the Eastern Communist states, including the Soviet
Union and East Germany. This policy of reconciliation was a
pragmatic and far-sighted reversal of the long held legalism
that reunification must precede détente. Although the Kiesinger government only partially succeeded in achieving its
objectives in Eastern Europe, it was widely assumed that
Czechoslovakia would soon recognize Bonn (following Rumania's precedent in 1967) in exchange for an expected extension of economic credits. The week before the intervention, a
West German official had announced that Bonn was willing to
declare the Munich Pact of 1938 "void from the outset," thus
paving the way for diplomatic relations, and Prague let it be
known that it was thinking of asking for credits from the
World Bank. Some have since argued that the Soviet intervention was the result of the success of Western—especially German—economic penetration of Eastern Europe and the
perceived need to arrest it.

It is likely that the *Ostpolitik,* although called into question, will not be abandoned, and that the search for the

normalization of relations with the East will be resumed despite the intervention, described by Brandt as "an earthquake that changed the European scenery, opening fissures and destroying bridges." There simply is no reasonable alternative. But the task will be far more difficult and little progress is likely before the Bundestag elections of September 1969. An anxious and frightened German people may then precipitate the breakup of the "Grand Coalition" by giving an absolute majority to the Christian Democrats. Past experience suggests that menacing policies from Moscow work to the detriment of the Social Democratic Party. In the general election of September 1957, nine months after the suppression of the Hungarian uprising, the party of Konrad Adenauer polled an absolute majority for the first, and so far only, time in German postwar history. Within the CDU, Chancellor Kurt Kiesinger has already come under attack from his right as a "détente illusionist" and the star of the more militant Franz-Josef Strauss is on the ascendant.

We must recognize that the danger does exist that an understandably frustrated and insecure West Germany might act in a manner which most Americans and West Europeans would consider rash and dangerous. German reunification appears as distant as ever. The expectations aroused by the German-French rapprochement of 1963 have not been realized. A return to heavy reliance on the United States, the policy of the Adenauer-Dulles years, does not seem to be feasible or in the American interest. Now the *Ostpolitik* has been dealt a serious setback. German anxieties have been activated by Czechoslovakia and by the repeated Russian claim to the residual right to move troops into the Federal Republic under Articles 53 and 107 of the United Nations Charter. Such a Germany may in time seek to come to an accommodation directly with the Soviet Union similar to the Rapallo Pact of 1922. This would not be an implausible outcome of a combination of fear and frustration. Conversely, West Germany, confident of her economic strength and her potential nuclear capability, might adopt an increasingly nationalistic policy. This I consider less likely, for German politicians know that

the reactions of the states both east and west of the Federal
Republic would make such an adventure self-defeating. Nevertheless, because of her apparent condemnation to continued
division and her geographical situation in the position most
exposed to the Soviet threat, Germany's dilemmas remain real
and vexing, and there is no way of predicting what may yet
happen.

Turning to the response of Washington to the Soviet intervention, we find a combination of firmness and flexibility.
Underneath this somewhat ambiguous response there seems
to be a pervasive wish that it had not happened—not solely
because of the aggression committed on the Czech people, or
even because of the erosion of American policy in Eastern
Europe. It is the necessary damping of Soviet-American relations on matters beyond Europe—in Southeast Asia, the
Middle East, and the arms race—that Administration officials
find especially galling. This was particularly true for a lame
duck President with deep felt ambitions for using the closing
days of his Administration to enlist Soviet assistance in a
Vietnam peace settlement, to ratify the non-proliferation
treaty, and to commence bilateral strategic missile limitation
talks.

The United States has reaffirmed its commitment to the
defense of Europe and has taken the lead in strengthening the
military capabilities of NATO; it could hardly do otherwise.
A White House announcement planned for the morning of
August 21, 1968, announcing an agreement to enter into
missile limitation talks with the Soviet Union was put into
deep freeze. Smarting from the accusation that Washington
did not take sufficient steps in the spring and early summer to
deter an intervention in Czechoslovakia, the Administration
issued a warning against Soviet intervention in Austria and
Yugoslavia. Under Secretary of State Nicholas Katzenbach
was dispatched to Belgrade to offer assurances of support to
President Tito should Moscow decide that the new "Brezhnev
doctrine," permitting interference in the internal affairs of
countries of the "Socialist Commonwealth," applied to Yugoslavia. Rumania, the only Warsaw Pact member not to par-

ticiapte in the invasion of Czechoslovakia, was rewarded with new agreements dealing with the peaceful uses of atomic energy and cultural exchange, unlike other Pact nations which had their prospective agreements cancelled.

American policy-makers are likely to feel a continuing interest in the preservation of some form of détente and bridge building. The risks of nuclear war are too great not to pursue policies leading to the relaxation of tension between the two camps. Recognizing that the Soviet Union should not be permitted to fully escape the consequences of Czechoslovakia, they have called for an augmentation—relatively minor —of NATO's military strength. But Washington will not "punish" Moscow, that is, attempt to make it pay the "price" for its offense, in such a manner as to cause self-inflicted injury. To interrupt the dialogue with Moscow, to refuse as a matter of principle to enter into any arms control agreements, would be to cut off one's nose to spite one's face. Efforts to achieve détente are not made for Russia's sake, or even primarily for the people of Eastern Europe, but are made in intelligent Western self-interest.

This is not to say that more attention should not be given to designing political strategies aimed towards deterring such occurrences as Czechoslovakia. We have some time ago tacitly accepted a Soviet sphere of influence in Eastern Europe just as we expect to have ours recognized in the Western hemisphere. But we should seek a declaratory policy which would create an element of ambiguity as to the consequences of "indecent" Soviet actions. Thus the Soviets would have no assurance that an "unacceptable" move on their part would not trigger a reaction, for example, a freeze on East-West trade, or an acceleration of strategic arms competition, which would make that move undesirable. The rules of the superpower détente game should be structured in such a way that neither power feels free to act in a totally unrestrained manner.

THE ATLANTIC AND WARSAW TREATIES

A discussion of the impact of the invasion of Czechoslovakia upon the continuing military confrontation of the forces
of NATO and the Warsaw Pact in Central Europe must take
into account both the military capabilities of the two alliances
and their perceived intentions. Looking first at forces-in-being,
it can be seen that the invasion may have significantly altered
the military balance in Central Europe. At the time of the
invasion, Soviet forces in East Germany and other Warsaw
Pact countries were increased from 22 to 32 divisions. The
ten divisions sent to Eastern Europe were replaced in the
western part of Russia by ten mobilized reserve divisions.[1]
This means that the Soviet Union has larger forces in Central
Europe than at any time since the early postwar period. The
seven Soviet divisions placed by agreement with Prague along
the Czechoslovak border of West Germany have a new forward deployment which increases the threat to NATO forces
by providing the ability to attack more quickly and with a
greater element of surprise. Moreover, and this is of considerable significance, the establishment of extensive communication and supply lines in Czechoslovakia has provided the
Soviet Union with the capability of moving additional forces
to the frontiers of West Germany. Many professional observers now believe that the military balance has been shifted
to the disadvantage of the West, although an unknown factor
pointing in the opposite direction is the extent to which the
Soviet position in Eastern Europe has become less secure, in
part because of the possible unreliability of the Czechoslovakian armed forces.

The significance of this becomes clearer when the new
Warsaw Pact capabilities are understood in the context of
NATO's strategy for the defense of Western Europe. In recent
times, NATO's contingency planning has been based upon the
assumption that there would be a warning period of several
weeks during a period of Soviet mobilization, and that this

would provide the time for American and British forces assigned to NATO, but held outside the European continent, to be returned promptly in time of crisis. The assumption of the availability of such a "political warning" was behind the 1967 decision to return 35,000 American NATO-assigned troops from Germany to the United States and it has guided NATO's reliance on mobilization arrangements rather than forces-in-being. The invasion of Czechoslovakia has now raised grave doubts about the wisdom of permitting NATO strategy to remain dependent upon a period of warning. We now know that "political warnings" might be ambiguous at best, that mobilization and plans for an invasion of West Germany could be hidden under the cloak of Warsaw Pact maneuvers, that the availability of reliable intelligence does not guarantee accurate evaluation of its meaning, and that Western governments, like all humans, might be inclined not to believe what they do not wish to hear.

Looking at Soviet intentions—and NATO's defense strategy is as much dependent upon an evaluation of Soviet intentions as on Soviet capabilities—we must now recognize that future Soviet military actions are less predictable than we had once assumed. This means that NATO's defense posture should be based on a greater range of uncertainty. This may be one of the lasting consequences of the Soviet intervention in Czechoslovakia. A new concept of Soviet unpredictability will make it more difficult for NATO countries to rationalize reductions in NATO's strength by the assumption of not only the availability of a warning time, but also an assumption of Soviet rationality and non-aggressive intentions.

Mention should also be made of the growing Soviet naval strength in the Mediterranean, for any strategic reappraisal of NATO forces after Czechoslovakia must take into account the increased Soviet presence there. Whatever be the rationale and purpose for the rapid buildup in the Mediterranean, there are fifty to sixty Soviet vessels in the area including a helicopter carrier, the *Moskva*. Soviet naval forces could become a threat to NATO supply lines, provide additional intervention capabilities, and attempt to engage allied forces, including American Polaris submarines, which now operate in the

Mediterranean. Certainly they do enhance the Soviet presence
in the Middle East and they tend to buttress political commitments which have been made to Arab states. Much of the
alarm which has of late been voiced, however, seems to me to
be either excessive or premature. The Soviet Mediterranean
fleet remains hopelessly outclassed by NATO naval forces. It
has no counterpart to the two powerful aircraft carriers of
the U.S. Sixth Fleet (each of which has 100 strike aircraft)
and indeed compares unfavorably with the Italian Navy in
numbers of ships. Moscow's fleet remains dependent for access to the Mediterranean and for its supply lines on passage
through either the Dardanelles or Gibraltar or the Suez Canal
once it is reopened. Two of these passageways are controlled
by NATO countries. Therefore fears that the Soviet Union
will be capable of "outflanking" the central front of NATO
are, in my opinion, exaggerated.

Despite what has happened in Czechoslovakia, NATO is
not likely to enter into a large-scale rearmament program, as
it did after the start of the Korean War. This is the judgment
that one must now make, in my view, following the first full
scale NATO ministerial meeting after the Soviet intervention
which was held in Brussels in mid-November 1968. The Alliance warned that any intervention directly or indirectly affecting the situation in Europe or in the Mediterranean "would
create an international crisis with grave consequences." Moscow was urged to refrain from force and interference. NATO
adopted a generally stiffer attitude towards the Soviet Union.
But there was no clarion call to arms in the form of massive
reinforcements. On the other hand, some countries have announced significant increases in defense expenditures.

The strengthening of NATO after Czechoslovakia will be
limited to suspension of expected reductions in manpower—
cutbacks which had been planned or intended by Belgium, the
Netherlands, West Germany, Canada and Britain—and improvements in the conventional equipment of the allied forces.
Some American units recently withdrawn from Europe will
be returned for military exercises but they will not remain
permanently. A series of measures will be taken to improve
the effectiveness of air, ground and naval weapons, but the

emphasis will be on quality rather than quantity. The ministers called for the improvement of contingency plans for a quick call-up and effective mobilization of reserve units in Western European countries. Many of these steps, however, appear to be somewhat cosmetic in nature.

This means that the local defense of Europe will more than ever be dependent upon the use of tactical nuclear weapons. Since early in the Kennedy Administration, American policy-makers have attempted to endow NATO with a policy of flexible, graduated response to a Soviet invasion so as to permit a conventional defense of Europe, at least at the early stages of a war, thus giving the enemy time for reflection. This policy was officially adopted by the Alliance in 1967. Such a policy, however, is dependent upon NATO forces sufficiently strong to give serious opposition to a conventional attack by the Warsaw Pact powers. Because of the French withdrawal from the Alliance's military structure—a step which cost the Alliance not only troops but much needed geography, because of the gradual reduction in NATO forces in recent years—and now because of the new forward deployment of Soviet troops, the defense of Europe by non-nuclear weapons is less plausible than ever.

The reasons for the somewhat muted response to the intervention are varied. None of the NATO nations sees a new clear, and imminent danger of a Soviet attack on the West. The country which feels the most threatened, West Germany, announced in November 1968 a 10,000 man increase in its army and a limited increase in its defense budget. Bonn is not likely to go further because of the risk that a massive increase in the German armed forces would be exploited by Moscow as evidence of German militarism, thus working against its *Ostpolitik* and its attempts to come to an agreement with the Soviet Union. Without a prevailing sense of imminent danger, the defense policies of most of the NATO countries are likely to continue to be shaped by considerations of financial stringency and balance of payments worries. It will take more than Czekoslovakia to shake Britain out of its unwillingness to reintroduce conscription. For those American defense planners who have for years been looking for ways to persuade the

Europeans to take on a greater share of providing for their own security, the Soviet intervention has almost been welcome. Prime Minister Trudeau of Canada has cautioned against overreacting and has even suggested that the Warsaw Pact may be weaker now than it was prior to the Soviet reinforcement in Eastern Europe because the Czechoslovak army and possibly other East European armies can no longer be counted upon as Russian allies in a military conflict. Undoubtedly important differences of views concerning NATO's détente policy and its force structure will reemerge with time.

Nevertheless, on balance NATO has been given an important psychological boost. The list of costs to the Soviets of the intervention in Czechoslovakia must include a strengthening, admittedly limited, of NATO. The Alliance's vitality has been revived just at the crucial time when it has first become legally permissible for members to withdraw.

LONG–RANGE IMPACT

What will be the long-range implications for the West of the Soviet intervention in Czechoslovakia? We must bear in mind that the impact of the Russian invasion of Prague will be similar in one sense to the Republican invasion of Washington—much depends on the next steps in the unknown future. The true meaning of the change in political environment will not be apparent for some time to come. Meanwhile, we run the risk of becoming immersed within our perceptions of what has happened thus far. We can, nevertheless, engage in some "educated" speculation.

1. In the United States there will be renewed attention to the problems of Europe and the Atlantic Community. In the past years of overwhelming attention to Southeast Asia and the Middle East, Europe has been half-forgotten or taken too much for granted. Although some may dispute this, certainly it is the impression of many Europeans that they have been ignored. Some Europeans see American mesmerization with Vietnam as having been at least partially responsible for

Czechoslovakia. They reason that if the United States had not shifted its primary focus from the European stage it would have paid greater attention to deterring the Soviet intervention. Czechoslovakia may now return American attention to its first priority, to the security area most vital to it. There will be a new concentration of energy and ideas on Atlantic problems.

2. The NATO alliance will take on increased importance and relevance. No longer will there by gloomy prophesies of the impending disintegration of the alliance. The maintenance of NATO's military structure will be seen as a continuing necessity of high order. The French attitude towards NATO may become less skeptical and it is highly unlikely that de Gaulle still entertains thoughts of leaving the alliance when this becomes possible in 1969, according to the NATO treaty. Already French officers are working far more closely with their Allied counterparts at Casteau. Within NATO there is likely to be increased consultation among its principal European members, particularly if France is cooperative. The idea has been raised of a "European Caucus" to foster closer economic, political and technological collaboration. The next officer to be appointed SACEUR might be a European general.

3. The strengthening of NATO following the invasion of Czechoslovakia will be tempered by a continuing United States desire to lighten its burdens in NATO through a relatively greater European contribution of manpower, resources and responsibilities. This means that unless East-West relations are again exacerbated there will be new pressures along the lines of the Mansfield Resolution and the Symington Amendment calling for a sharp reduction in United States forces in Europe.

4. Czechosolovakia will serve as a sharp reminder of the European dependence upon American nuclear weapons and will also increase Europe's reliance upon them. Europeans have once again been forced to recognize that their security, in the final analysis, rests with the American nuclear deterernt. NATO forces, because of the increase in Soviet forces and their new forward deployment in Bohemia, may be compelled to use tactical nuclear weapons at an earlier stage.

5. A strategy will need to be designed to try to prevent further Soviet interventions such as Czechoslovakia. This crisis has once again demonstrated the weakness of nuclear weapons. The difficulty with a Western defense policy based on nuclear deterrence is that it has a substantial amount of self-deterrence built into it. Therefore it has little credibility outside the NATO area, even when applied to such "grey areas" as Yugoslavia and Austria. Greater attention should be given to techniques of verbal interposition and to mechanisms such as the cancellation of commercial, scientific, and cultural cooperation. These could be used in such a way as to deter the Soviets from an aggressive move by threatening a "price" to be paid. A guiding principle in such a strategy might be to impose upon Moscow an element of uncertainty as to what the consequences of "unacceptable" actions would be.

6. Soviet-American relations may be entering into a new phase which will have important consequences for détente and for the future of Europe. It may be that Czechoslovakia is only one manifestation of the frost that is returning to the Cold War on a wide range of issues. The Soviet Union, for reasons of its own about which one can speculate, may welcome a period of Cold War confrontation in which it could pursue repressive policies and emphasize ideological conformity, and during which the control of events in Eastern Europe could under no circumstances slip between its fingers. This would undoubtedly dampen the European détente and help bloc the initiatives of *Ostpolitik* and a Gaullist type of foreign policy.

Simultaneously, the Soviet Union may wish to "normalize" its relations with the United States on a series of issues on which the two superpowers appear to have common interests. One of these would be negotiations on arms control measures. Such a double-edged approach, if accepted by the United States, could lead to serious repercussions among America's allies if they are made to feel by-passed and neglected. A true détente between the two nuclear superpowers could hardly be faulted, for it would measurably reduce world tensions. But a so-called "condominium" in which the two superpowers police the world by tacit agreement, retaining important elements of ideological and military confrontation, would tend to erode relations between the United States and Western Europe.

7. Particularly in a "condominium" world, but even without it, I expect to see important transformations on the European scene. Let us discuss some possibilities, not all of which are mutually exclusive. In the relatively short run I would not be surprised at some significant adjustments in French foreign policy. This would include a rapprochement between Paris and Washington, and also between Paris and London.

The de Gaulle regime was shaken to its roots by the events of 1968. The students' and workers' riots in May, revealing widespread discontent, snapped the stability of the Fifth Republic and, by de Gaulle's own admission, are responsible for the economic disorder of the country today. The run on the franc has cost France half of its reserves and there is no assurance that the fiscal measures undertaken will avert a future monetary crisis. Czechoslovakia has undermined the belief that France could help create a Europe stretching from the Atlantic to the Urals. The increased Soviet presence on France's southern frontier in the Mediterranean, and in particular the rapidly expanding Russian influence in Algeria, has deeply disturbed French officials. These events, especially the suddenness with which most of them came, revealed the de Gaulle regime to be extraordinarily brittle. The austerity measures which now lie ahead, the failure to provide for the promised "participation" in industry, and the reduction in funds for educational reform could once again provoke action on the barricades. De Gaulle can well be concerned that on the second round the outcome may not be as favorable.

Therefore the Gaullist regime may see value in ameliorating relations with the United States. The advent of a new American administration will give him the opportunity. De Gaulle and Nixon have maintained an excellent relationship since the 1950's, based perhaps on their common experience of having spent long winters in the political wilderness. Paris is appreciative of the assistance received during the monetary crisis and the French challenge to the dollar, which stirred so

much resentment in the United States, has been ended. The
Vietnam negotiations in Paris have erased one irritant in the
past relationship and the partial return to NATO will
smoothen another. The road is clear to putting Franco-American relations on a new tack and may well tempt President
Nixon.

8. Similarly, relations between Paris and London may
be entering into a new era. This would be the result of a
revised perception of Germany by the French. Germany is
growing in self-confidence and economic power at just the
same time that France's policy in the East has been check-
mated. It can be argued that with France's decline in recent
times and Germany's ascendancy, a fundamental realignment
of power will take place. Primacy in Europe may pass from
Paris to Bonn. The Federal Republic today has the largest
army in Western Europe, the most bountiful stocks of gold,
and the highest gross national product in Europe. The Gaullist
regime may therefore relax its attitude towards British entry
into the Common Market in order to restore the balance. But it
should be borne in mind that the calculation that might one
day make the French willing to let Britain into Europe is
precisely the calculation that might make the Germans want
to keep it out. The Germans know perfectly well that with the
United Kingdom in the Common Market, the balance of power
may swing against them, even if not necessarily on all issues.

9. Assistance in nuclear technology may be the key to
unlocking many of the above noted possibilities. The expen-
sive and technologically ambitious French nuclear program for
building hardened underground intercontinental ballistic missiles and submarine launched missiles and equipping them
with thermonuclear warheads is in financial straits. The
United States may reverse its policy of recent years and provide technological assistance to France. This could be achieved
within the limits of the 1958 American atomic energy legisla-
tion without requiring the explicit approval of the Congress.
Another possibility would be for Britain to enter into a col-
laborative arrangement with France. In the past the necessity
of Washington's prior approval for this has been one of the
impediments. But time has been gradually diminishing the

number and value of "American" secrets in Britain's posses-
sion and even if the United States should retain a negative
attitude on British-French collaboration, London may be
tempted to proceed with it anyway.

10. The invasion of Czechoslovakia, particularly if it is
followed by a further deterioration of West European-Com-
munist bloc relations, could give new life to some old ideas
about European unity. It can be argued that a greater measure
of coordination in European foreign and defense policies
would add to the deterrence capability of the West in fore-
stalling future Soviet interventions in Eastern Europe. Having now seen the weakness of their past uncoordinated
approaches to détente, the West Europeans may attempt to
develop a common policy toward the Soviet Union and with
respect to a German settlement. Furthermore, should Soviet-
American relations lead to a "condominium" world, the West
Europeans may recognize and act upon the concept that only
in unity will they be able to exercise real influence upon the
two superpowers. On the other hand, it is also possible that
Western Europe, reacting against a "condominium" world,
would turn inward, withdrawing from world affairs and
adopting a position of neutrality. In such a case, the separate
West European countries might follow foreign policies characterized by narrow nationalism and privatism. There would
be a breakdown and dispersal of common West European interests and we could expect individual countries to make their
private, bilateral accommodations with the Soviet Union.

11. "Détente is not just a matter of smiles and soap. In
present circumstances, it is much more a matter of reducing
the world's common perils by properly safeguarded measures
of arms control." [2]

The impact of the invasion of Czechoslovakia on arms
control has been, and may for some time remain, considerable.
The adoption of arms control measures usually requires some
mutual trust, which is probably now more lacking in Soviet-
American relations than at any time since the Cuban missile
crisis.

The nuclear non-proliferation treaty has been delivered a
severe blow. Prior to August 21, 1968, all indications pointed

to a quick and relatively painless ratification of the treaty in the United States Senate. Even after American ratification in 1969, the delay—the import of the delay—will have been damaging to the chances of the treaty's being adopted by the largest number of states. Those opposed to the treaty in such critical nations as West Germany, Italy, India, Japan, Israel and Brazil have had their resistance fortified not only by the Russian action, but by the American delay. World-wide ratification of such a contentious treaty can be a highly dynamic and psychological process which may depend considerably upon the forces of political momentum. The sudden display of self-doubts by the principal supporter of such a measure may result in a snowballing effect out of proportion to the original doubts. Support for the treaty in West Germany has, understandably, greatly diminished. The Christian Democrats, never enamored of the treaty, are increasing their resistance to it and the Social Democrats, though still favoring the treaty, have become less enthusiastic about it. A number of countries have said they will not submit the treaty to their parliaments for ratification until after the United States has completed its own ratification procedures. Within the Political Committee of the United Nations General Assembly a resolution was offered in late 1968 which would re-open for debate many of the old questions concerning the provisions of the treaty on disarmament, peaceful uses of atomic energy and security guarantees.

The adoption of proposals for an East-West agreement on the mutual reduction of forces in Central Europe can be ruled out for some time. At the Reykjavik meeting of NATO ministers in June, 1968, it was agreed that proposals be studied for a balanced and gradual reduction of the military forces of the NATO and Warsaw Pact organizations, to be accomplished in reciprocal manner. It is not likely that such proposals will receive serious attention in the immediate future. Nevertheless, we can expect to see a continuing interest in the search for a new European security system. The invasion of Czechoslovakia has raised doubts that the Soviet Union will be interested in any European security system that does not permit it to retain a firm grip on Eastern Europe. If in the future, however, Moscow finds its position in Eastern Europe increasingly untenable, it may welcome the opportunity to negotiate a European security system with the West in order to stabilize its Western borders.

The commencement of discussion between the United States and the Soviet Union on the mutual limitation of offensive and defensive strategic missiles has been delayed by the Soviet intervention. As mentioned earlier, it is widely believed that an announcement on the initiation of such talks had been scheduled by President Johnson for the morning of the same day that news of the Soviet action reached Washington. Proponents of delay have argued that such bilateral negotiations would imply tacit acceptance of the Soviet aggression and would alarm many of America's allies. Nevertheless, I believe that the considerable common interest in the discussion of the possibility of strategic missile limitations is likely to return this important arms control issue to the forefront at the proper time and under appropriate circumstances.

In the long run, the events in Czechoslovakia may be seen to have stimulated the arms race. The Soviet Union has been made to appear more unpredictable and aggressive than some had thought. The terms nuclear "superiority" and nuclear "parity" are difficult to define and perhaps meaningless; nonetheless they have acquired a certain currency in public discussions. It may be that those who support "parity" have had their position weakened by the Soviet behavior. There is no indication, however, that clear cut "superiority" in strategic nuclear weapons can or would provide the political leverage to prevent similar Soviet interventions in Eastern Europe.

Finally, the negative impact of Czechoslovakia upon the nonproliferation treaty and upon the expected strategic missile limitation discussions raises the question whether more thought should not be given to the possibility and means by which some arms control issues might be "uncoupled" from other issues in the East-West confrontation. One can postulate that there may be a range of issues of such transcending importance to the entire international system that every effort should be made to keep discussions on such items separate from the normal political confrontations of international politics. Such items would typically include issues which affect the safety of large numbers of people or large parts of the world environment, such as the development and dispersion of weapons of mass destruction, the use of chemical and biological weapons, the control of outer space and the seabed, and the pollution of the air and the sea. The concept would be that if a general understanding were reached that issues of high priority to the world system, however defined, should be "divorced" from the normal interplay of conflicting national interests, governments would not feel obliged to call off discussions or negotiations on such issues in order to show displeasure.

Naturally there may be occasions when governments agree to "uncouple" an issue and then change their mind. For example, with relation to the non-proliferation treaty, a West European government may now feel that as a result of Czechoslovakia it should maintain its option of acquiring nuclear weapons. On the other hand, a prior "uncoupling" probably would have reduced the pressures in the United States following the Soviet intervention for going slow on the ratification of the treaty. The concept of "uncoupling" may well be Pollyanna-like, for it can be argued that it is politically naive to attempt this type of separation. Certainly the failure of international law to provide a world system of law argues against the rationality of states in accepting what is best for the entire community of nations. Moreover, it may be inconsistant with both the Soviet view of conflict and the European political tradition. Nevertheless, as arms races continue and technology produces ever greater and more efficient means of destruction, nations may see the value of differentiating still further their national security policies. Not all governments will decide that self-confidence, image, and prestige requires them to retaliate against a hostile step by another government in such a manner as to inflict self-punishment. If there is any merit in the idea of "uncoupling," then study should be undertaken to determine whether it might best be attempted by tacit agreements or institutional mechanisms, and if the latter, what the varieties and advantages of various institutional "uncoupling" mechanisms might be.

*   *   *

The course of history is not unlike the course of the individual as he passes through a lifetime. Some occurrences or longer term developments may be the result of a deliberate choice or of accidental events. Others are more the product of relatively inflexible formative forces. So it is also in the life of nations and in their relationships with one another. In looking back a year later upon the foregoing prognosis of the Western response to the Soviet intervention in Czechoslovakia, and in examining what has transpired since the forecast made shortly after the Soviet action, it might be informative to ask: What has taken place as the result of chance and the emergence of new personalities on the center stage? What has been the product of broad, relatively immutable, historical forces?

Turning first to the role of historical accident, we can see that the outcome of general elections has fairly significantly affected the policies of the Federal Republic of Germany, France and the United States. Perhaps the most exciting and consequential change has taken place in West Germany, where the Social Democrats in alliance with the Free Democrats have taken the helm from a party which had been in power since the beginning of the post-war era. Willy Brandt began his chancellorship with a series of rapid measures which could hardly have been expected from a new Kiesinger government or even a renewed CDU coalition with the SPD. These included the quick signing of the nuclear non-proliferation treaty and the upward revaluation of the mark by even a greater margin than had been anticipated in financial circles. Both actions were bold, courageous ones of the type that are most readily made in the receptive atmosphere of a new administration. Brandt also deserves much credit for the agreement worked out at the Hague in December 1969 by the six European Common Market members to be prepared for negotiations in the summer of 1970 on the admission of Britain and other applicants. He appears to have taken a much stronger line in dealing with France on this matter than any previous West German Chancellor.

In France a relatively unimportant and unnecessary referendum in April 1969 on the creation of administrative regions and on the reform of the Senate led to the unexpectedly sudden return of de Gaulle to Colombey-les-deux-Eglises. It is still too early to estimate with any confidence the nature of Georges Pompidou's own policies, since it will take time for the image of his own authority to emerge from its Gaullist heritake. We can nevertheless already observe a more modest vision of France's place in the world and a new attitude towards the question of British admission into the Common Market. French military cooperation within NATO is also slowly being restored. The change of administration in the United States heralded a somewhat more tough-minded approach to arms control issues and probably delayed, though not greatly, their policy implementation. A President-elect Humphrey might have acceded to Lyndon Johnson's desire to submit the nuclear non-proliferation treaty to the Senate and to commence the strategic arms limitation talks before the end of the latter's term in office.

But it is the continuity of policies, rather than their alteration, that is most interesting, and their very predictability that is most striking. Quite clearly the sweep of historical forces imposes impressive restraints upon the range of what some professional futurologists refer to as "alternative futures." The Nixon Administration has renewed American attention to Western Europe, as shown by the President's trip to Europe shortly after his inauguration. What new policies have resulted, or which old ones have been reoriented and how, is however, far less apparent. As predicted, the strengthening of NATO after the Russian action in Czechoslovakia has been severely limited by budgetary restraints and a widespread disbelief in a real Soviet military threat. Senator Mansfield has once again taken up the call for a reduction of American ground forces in Western Europe, and Prime Minister Trudeau's reexamination of Canada's commitment has resulted in a decision to scale down the Canadian contribution to NATO by fifty percent. Partially in the expectation of a reduced level of troops available to SACEUR, the Nuclear Planning Group has undertaken an examination of the doctrine for the use of tactical nuclear weapons, a step which was made more urgent by the new forward deployment of Soviet forces in Czechoslovakia.

There is a deep American interest in maintaining civil relations with the Soviet Union which clearly does transcend the anger and frustration caused in the West by the demagogic and brutal Soviet action in Czechoslovakia. The two nuclear superpowers have been characterized as scorpions caught in a bottle, able to sting one another only at the price of death. Because of the need to assure some level of strategic stability, the United States has decided that it is in its own overriding self-interest to enter into quite intimate negotiations with the Soviet Union in the limitation of strategic nuclear armaments. For reasons of world stability the United States has also ratified the nuclear nonproliferation treaty. The knee-jerk reaction of halting ratification of the treaty after the events of August 1968 has been overcome and there is now no more talk of "punishing" the Soviet Union.

The fundamental interests of West Germany have reemerged in a similar manner. The attempt to develop better relations with Eastern Europe and the Soviet Union, momentarily discredited by the Soviet invasion, has been once again taken up. Thus we see in the Moscow negotiations on a treaty for the mutual renunciation of force, and in discussions between Bonn and East European countries on credit arrangements, a new version of the only momentarily discredited *Ostpolitik*. The gropings of Willy Brandt for a new understanding with the Communist nations is necessary if progress is to be made towards an eventual settlement of the problem of Germany. There is no alternative, and most Germans know it, so that within Germany the tragedy of Czechslovakia was not seen as evidence of the ultimate failure of *Ostpolitik*.

France is the nation whose vision towards the East has

been most impaired by the Soviet intervention in Czechoslovakia and we see only minor signs of a renewal of active
diplomacy with the Warsaw Pact nations. This temporarily
less active role must be seen, however, as part of a generally
lower diplomatic posture. Correctly reading into the past dissatisfaction with de Gaulle a growing concern for economic
and social problems at home, Pompidou has decided to concentrate on domestic priorities. The reform of the universities,
and even the "quality of life" of the individual Frenchman,
is now a matter of governmental concern. The French economy
has shown itself to be less healthy than once assumed. The
devaluation of the franc, taken with the upward reevaluation
of the mark, has been seen by some in France as an indication
of a shift in political as well as economic power from France
to Germany. This explains in part the more flexible attitude
toward British entry into the Common Market, since it is
thought that Britain may in the future be needed in order to
balance Germany.

In the perspective of history the Western response to the
Soviet intervention in Czechoslovakia is likely to be read as
a muted one, far less energizing than might have been a clear
attack upon a nation which we were committed to defend, as
in the case of South Korea. The events of August 1968 clearly
did not cause a refraction of the historical forces at play
within the West. Perhaps the chief impact of the Czech tragedy is that it will have forced us to modify our perceptions
on the possibilities for détente, and will have made us less
hopeful but wiser. We must be less optimistic as to what we
can expect in the way of Soviet willingness to permit a relaxation within Eastern Europe.. And we must be more realistic
as to what NATO members will freely undertake in order to
safeguard their security, barring a direct threat to their survival. Meanwhile we must persist in the quest for an East-
West reconciliation in Europe.

NOTES

1. On August 20–21 the Soviet Union and its four Warsaw Pact Allies moved 25 divisions, or approximately 250,000 men, into Czechoslovakia. Eight Soviet divisions moved from East Germany, eleven from the western part of the Soviet Union and four from Hungary. One additional airborne division was flown from the Soviet Union to take over Prague's air field and other facilities. In addition. three Polish divisions and smaller units from Hungary, Bulgaria, and East Germany took part in the invasion.

2. "The Half-Built Bridges," *The Economist*, September 14, 1968.

Military Intervention by the Great Powers: The Rules of the Game

by Andrew M. Scott

NATIONAL SOVEREIGNTY AND THE NORM OF NON-INTERVENTION

Since its birth, the nation-state system has been characterized by periodic military interventions by the great powers. Yet the phenomenon of intervention has received very little systematic attention. Individual cases of intervention have been examined and have usually been lamented, but there has not been much concern for the identification of regularities in interventionist behavior. This paper examines military interventions by the two great powers—the United States and the Soviet Union—since the end of World War II.[1]

Nations that are a part of an international system must produce norms and doctrines that justify the system and the way that it operates. The central doctrine supporting the system is, of course, that of "national sovereignty," whereby each nation-state is deemed to be sovereign and obedient to no authority beyond itself. Anything that intereferes with sovereignty would tend to undermine the foundations of the system.

Thus intervention of one nation-state in the affairs of another represents a clear denial of the principle of national sovereignty. If sovereignty is regarded as "good," as it is, then intervention must obviously be regarded as "bad."

The norm of nonintervention is a stabilizing factor on the international scene. The two predominant powers have frequently proclaimed their attachment to the principle of nonintervention. As that principle is currently conceived, however, it is evidently not one that they can live with in practice.[2] The two great powers intervene in the affairs of other nations in a variety of ways and on a continuing basis.[3] The form of intervention that most clearly contravenes the principle of nonintervention is military intervention, and each of the great powers has resorted to it on occasion.

II. SPHERES OF INFLUENCE

Under what circumstances would one of the predominant powers engage in military intervention? During the period under study, bipolarity has been a prominent feature of the international system. This has meant, among other things, that each of the predominant powers had its own sphere of influence; that there was frequent competition for the support of countries that were not aligned; and that military intervention by either power would be of interest to the other. During this period interventions frequently had to do with the maintenance of extension of one or the other of the spheres of influence.

This raises the question of how spheres of influence are established, how they change, and how their extent is determined. The boundaries of a sphere are tested by probes from the challenging power, in a variety of forms—overt, covert, political, economic, cultural, or military, of which the last is the most dangerous. A probe can be countered by a response on the part of the nation whose sphere is being probed, through a pledge, a threat, a promise, military action, economic aid, and so on.

Probes are the equivalent of test cases in law. They determine the credibility of the claims to a sphere of influence. If probes are not met firmly in a given area, a question is automatically raised as to whether that area should still be considered as within a sphere of influence. If the probes are firmly rebuffed, however, rebuff serves to establish, or to reconfirm, the boundaries of a sphere of influence. Khrushchev's effort to locate ballistic missiles in Cuba probed the determination of the United States to maintain its sphere of interest around Cuba, which the powerful American response affirmed. If the United States had not responded firmly to that probe, the entire notion of the Western Hemisphere as an American sphere of influence might have collapsed.

A great power may reconfirm the features of its sphere of influence by actions that it initiates as well as by its response to probes. The American intervention in the Dominican Republic is an example of such an action. The Soviet invasion of Hungary (1956) and Czechoslovakia (1968) confirmed these countries' position in the Soviet sphere. The ability of the Soviet Union to extract from the Rumanian Government an agreement to allow Soviet troops to conduct military maneuvers on its soil reconfirms the location of Rumania within the Soviet sphere.

A nation-state can use a probe to challenge the sphere of influence of another power and to incorporate an area into its own sphere. If one of the great powers extends a series of probes into an uncommitted country, and if those probes are not rebuffed by that country or by the other great power, then it may be considered to have brought that country into its own sphere of interest. For example, if the Soviet Union extended probes into Austria that were not rebuffed by Austria and the Western nations, Austria's position as an uncommitted country would soon be questioned. To be sure, the status of a country is not always clear-cut and a country may be moved into or out of a sphere of influence by degrees.

A sphere of influence can never be said to have been established once and for all. As we said above, a given area remains within a sphere of influence only as long as the dominant nation in that sphere rebuffs probes or reconfirms its sphere by its own initiatives. If a sphere is not maintained, it ceases to be accepted as a sphere by some other power. If an area is known to be in a given sphere of influence and there are no indications that the dominant power has weakened, that area may not be probed very often. A sphere of influence may be regarded as stabilized when 1) the defending power will respond firmly and reliably to probes and 2) when the other power understands that the first will do so.

The norm of nonintervention, to the extent that it actually is a factor in discouraging intervention, helps to stabilize existing spheres of influence. The response to a probe also is a stabilizing factor. The probe itself, however, is an instrument of change. In this perspective the concept of a "sphere of influence" becomes dynamic rather than static. Over a sufficiently long span of time a sphere of influence can take shape, undergo change, and suffer eventual dissolution. The concept of a "sphere of influence" thus has an obvious utility for the analyst of international politics but because of its static appearance, it has proved resistant to effective use.

RULES OF THE GAME

If one of the great powers should consider setting aside the principle of nonintervention in favor of a military action in some country, that would not mean that its behavior was moving from the realm of the understandable into the realm of the totally unpredictable. There are certain "rules of the game" pertaining to intervention that the great powers are likely to observe, thus giving their behavior a degree of predictability.

The norm contains an *ethical* element since that which is thought to be helpful to the international system is viewed as "good" and behavior which interferes with its workings is deemed to be wicked. The rules of the game, on the other hand, reflect the *interests* of the great powers. The rules have not been established by an external authority, or formally agreed upon; there is simply tacit agreement concerning their substance. They are not invariably followed, but if they are at all, it is because they are simple and appear to accord with the interests of each nation.

The rules of the game are not fixed but evolve over time with changing circumstances. They are made and unmade by the players as they play. A rule that is not agreed upon by both players is no rule at all. Periods of rapid change, therefore, are dangerous because there is an uncertainty concerning the substance of the rules and the way in which the great powers will apply them. The rules of the game are accepted by the two active countries in the subsystem as the intervention rules for the system. Since these rules are the rules of a special subsystem they need not accord with the formulations of international law or the rules applying to other subsystems. Indeed, it is likely that the rules the super-powers abide by in their interventionary behavior may be distasteful to other nations.[4]

I will examine three types of military intervention by the great powers. "Intra-bloc intervention" refers to military intervention by a great power in its own sphere of influence. "Inter-bloc intervention" involves military intervention by one of the great powers in an area that is within the sphere of influence of the other great power. "Extra-bloc intervention" involves intervention by a great power in an area that is not in its sphere of influence or in the sphere of influence of the other power.

Analytically these three types of intervention are clear-cut and distinct, almost ideal types. In practice, however, it is not always easy to fit a concrete example of intervention neatly into one or the other of the categories.

INTRA-BLOC INTERVENTION

The most important rule to be followed by a nation that it is intervening in its own sphere of influence is to act in such a way as to minimize the danger of a direct confrontation with the other great power and to facilitate the other power's acceptance of the action. In order to minimize the danger of great power confrontation, there are a number of subordinate rules that the intervening nation is likely to observe.

1. In its pronouncements it will minimize the extent of the intervention.
2. It will minimize the precedent-breaking nature of the action. In an interview at the time of the Dominican Republic intervention, for example, Secretary Rusk denied that the intervention represented "a departure from long-established policy."
3. All pronouncements will stress the temporary and short-term nature of the intervention. Again intervention in the Dominican Republic can be cited.
4. The intervening nation will try to arrange to be invited to intervene by the government of the country in which the intervention is to take place. If the power has been invited in, intervention presumably ceases to be intervention and becomes a friendly act of assistance. The United States was invited to intervene in the Dominican Republic and the Soviet Union arranged to be invited into Hungary. The Soviet Government initially claimed to have been invited to send troops into Czechoslovakia as well.
5. The intervening country will try to achieve a speedy victory. Because the political costs associated with a large-scale military intervention are very little greater than those associated with a small-scale intervention, the intervening power should employ sufficient military force to do the job quickly and thoroughly. The reason for the emphasis on speed is obvious: If fighting is prolonged the behavior of other nations becomes less predictable. They may find it difficult to avoid the temptation to become politically involved. A quick kill, however, presents other nations with a *fait accompli.* The Soviet intervention in Czechoslovakia accords with this rule, for an estimated (by Western sources) 650,000 troops were involved. The Soviet Union apparently learned the lesson of too little and too late during the first phase of its military intervention in Hungary. The United States injected approximately 35,000 troops into the tiny Dominican Republic.
6. To give the appearance of legitimacy to its intervention the intervening country may try to associate other countries in its sphere of influence with the interventionist action. The Soviet Union arranged to have its troops accom-

panied by the troops of four other Warsaw Pact countries during its invasion of Czechoslovakia. After its intervention in the Dominican Republic the United States sought, and received, endorsement of this action by the Organization of American States.

If the great power involved feels that it can avoid military intervention, it will probably seek to do so. The use of nonmilitary means of intervention makes it easier to disguise the element of coercion involved and is a far less obvious and disagreeable type of action. Military intervention is the most obvious form of intervention, and it does not leave the other great power the option of minimizing it or ignoring it. The Soviet Union has been "intervening" in the internal affairs of Czechoslovakia since before the coup in 1948, and the prolongation of the intervention had generated something akin to legitimacy. If the Soviet Union had been able to reestablish its control over the country without relying upon troops, the event would have been lamented, and the Soviet Union would have been castigated but Soviet action would have produced far less concern abroad.

The rules noted above apply to the intervening nation. There are also rules to be observed by the other great power.

7. When a great power is confronted with military intervention by the other great power in the latter's sphere of influence, it will express moral outrage and will take various symbolic actions such as offering resolutions in international bodies.
8. It may consider a variety of relatively mild actions designed to embarrass or punish the offending nation for its action.
9. It will not treat the action as a *casus belli*. Neither of the great powers is prepared to go to war over actions that the other takes in its own sphere of influence. Each recognizes that developments in the other's sphere are far more important to the other nation than to it and that the other nation is therefore prepared to run greater risks than it is in connection with those developments. This means that intra-bloc interventions will normally be unilateral rather

than competitive, as was the case when Russia intervened in East Germany, Hungary, and Czechoslovakia, and the United States intervened in the Dominican Republic.

INTER-BLOC INTERVENTION

The central rule of the game in the case of inter-bloc intervention is simple and clear-cut: Do not intervene, if you want to avoid war. The logic is an extension of the rules applied in an intra-bloc situation (IV 9, above). That is, a nation does not respond militarily to the initiatives of the other power in the sphere of influence of that power and it does not undertake military initiatives in the sphere of the other. This rule is obvious to both powers and will probably be ignored only in the case of a misunderstanding or if the challenging power is purposely leading to war. The United States did not respond militarily to the Soviet interventions in Hungary and Czechoslovakia because it recognized the danger of war. The same realization points to the avoidance of any military initiative by the United States in the Soviet sphere of influence.
— Because the rule forbids military intervention in the sphere of the other there are not many examples of such intervention to be cited. The Soviet effort to locate ballistic missiles in Cuba is an exception and apparently arose out of a misunderstanding. Because the United States allowed a pro-Soviet government to exist in Cuba and did not follow through and overwhelm Cuba at the time of the Bay of Pigs incident, Khrushchev appears to have concluded that President Kennedy was not prepared to maintain the American sphere of interest by strong action. There an effort to establish a missile basis in Cuba seemed to him to be a reasonable probe—offering potentially great gains and not involving commensurate risks. When Khrushchev was persuaded to ignore the rule against military intervention in the sphere of influence of the other power he precipitated what was possibly the most direct and tense showdown between the Soviet Union and the United States since the end of World War II.

Khrushchev did not understand that the United States might hesitate to intervene militarily in its own sphere of interest and yet be perfectly clear in its mind that it could not tolerate the military intervention of another power in that sphere. The United States was not ready to act officially against Cuba in an intra-bloc situation but it was instantly ready to act when the Soviet missile initiative created an inter-bloc situation. Instead of applying the rules pertaining to intra-bloc intervention, President Kennedy was forced to apply the rules pertaining to inter-bloc intervention. A great power can choose to intervene or not to intervene in its own sphere but, unless it is prepared to watch the dissolution of its sphere, it cannot fail to respond to the military intervention of the other power in its sphere. President's Kennedy's speech of October 22, 1962 made it clear that Soviet intervention "in an area well known to have a special and historical relationship to the United States" was a deliberately provocative and unjustified change in the status quo which cannot be accepted by this country, if our courage and our commitments are ever to be trusted again by either friend or foe.

EXTRA-BLOC INTERVENTION

Extra-bloc intervention covers a broad spectrum of cases, everything from intervention in a country that it thoroughly detached from either bloc to intervention in a country that has a special relationship with one of the powers even though it is not in the sphere of influence of that power. The rules are ambiguous.

10. The more important a great power deems an uncommitted area to be, the more seriously it will regard military intervention in that area by the other power. An area may be considered important to a great power because of what that area can add to the great power's strength or because of the necessity of denying the support of that area to the other great power.

11. The more closely an uncommitted area is associated with a sphere of influence the less likely it is that the other great power will take serious offense at the first power's military intervention in that area. That is, the second power perceives the situation as being almost an intra-bloc situation and is therefore prepared to act in almost the way that it would act in an intra-bloc situation.

12. The more closely an uncommitted area is associated with a given sphere of influence the greater will be the concern of that power if the other power should attempt a military intervention. That is, it perceives the situation as similar to the inter-bloc situation and it reacts in a somewhat similar way.

There is obviously a vast grey area between situations that are "almost" intra-bloc and those that are "almost" inter-bloc, and the opportunity for dangerously divergent perceptions by the great powers is great. One of the great powers might regard a third country as almost in its sphere of influence and therefore be prepared to act with the freedom appropiate to an intra-bloc situation. The other great nation might perceive the third nation as uncommitted or in *its* sphere of influence. For example, for geographical and historical reasons, the Soviet Union feels that Yugoslavia is within its sphere of influence. Following the NATO ministerial meeting in November, 1968, however, Secretary Rusk announced that Yugoslavia and Austria fall within the Western sphere of security interests. (Marshal Tito responded by stating that Yugoslavia was not in anyone's sphere of influence and, indeed, did not recognize such spheres.) Given such varying perceptions of Yugoslavia's position, the possibility of a dangerous confrontation is substantial. The danger of a military confrontation between the great powers is not great in intra-bloc situations since the rules are clear and each nation knows what is expected of it. In extra-bloc situations, however, neither may know what to expect of the other.

Several of the intra-bloc rules also apply in extra-bloc cases. For example, if at all possible the intervening country will try to arrange to be invited to intervene, as was the United States in Lebanon in 1958. The intervening nation will want to stress the temporary and special nature of the intervention, and will want to complete the military part of the operation as quickly as possible in order to hold down the level of risk.

THE DECISION TO INTERVENE

The rules of the game may permit a nation to intervene in a given case but they do not command it to do so. What kind of calculations might decision-makers make as they consider the merits of intervention?

Governments will normally consider, as best they can, the costs and gains associated with the proposed intervention. In a given situation there may be a number of different intervention options to be considered, each with a set of benefits and a set of costs associated with it. The decision-makers would have to assess the probable costs of intervention, the probable benefits of intervention, the probable costs of nonintervention, the probable benefits of nonintervention. That is, they would have to calculate the probable *net* benefits (or losses) to be derived from intervention and the probable *net* benefits (or losses) to be derived from nonintervention, which should indicate *whether* the decision should be made for or against intervention. Changes in these values over time must also be incorporated to indicate *when* intervention should or should not occur. When the element of time is incorporated the variety of the possible relationships become apparent. A favorable cost balance now may be reversed some time later, and vice versa. Decision-makers will not find it easy to make calculations of this kind, however, for costs and benefits cannot be quantified with any great precision. Nevertheless it would be possible for them to think in general terms about the relationships between costs and benefits.

To say that the rules of the game are observed because they incorporate elements of self-interest means that these rules must be justifiable in terms of the costs and benefits that would be derived from adherence to them. Why, for example,

should an intervening nation seek a clean, quick kill? Because
this course of action is likely to minimize long-term costs, for
costs associated with intervention increase with the passage
of time. Why should a nation try to arrange to be invited to
intervene? Because this would cut the costs and risks associated with the intervention. Why should a great power not
respond militarily to military intervention by the other power
in its own sphere for interest? Because the benefits from the
action might be slight and the costs might be great.

A rough cost/benefit analysis can be applied to decisions
by the United States and the Soviet Union to intervene militarily in other countries. The decision to intervene will turn
on the analysis of the following factors: 1) the existing situation; 2) its seriousness (i.e., present costs); 3) probable future seriousness (i.e., future costs); 4) the policy options
available and the effectiveness of each option; 5) present
and/or future costs and benefits associated with the use of
each option. These factors can be used to analyse the Soviet
decision in Czechoslovakia and elsewhere in Eastern Europe.

First, the Soviet Union is willing to tolerate policy deviation on the part of an Eastern European country as long as
that deviation does not endanger Soviet control of the Communist Party, the government, and basic governmental policy
in that country. In Hungary in 1956 and in East Germany in
1953, the Party/government apparatus could no longer control
events in the country. In Czechoslovakia in 1968 the Party/
government apparatus *would* no longer follow Soviet direction.
It is loss of control of the situation by the Soviet Union that
leads to the question of intervention being raised.

Next to be considered is the estimate of the seriousness of
the situation. Loss of control in a country does not automatically bring military intervention. For several years the Soviet
Union lacked adequate control over the policies of the Rumanian Government, yet did not intervene militarily in
Rumania. The explanation for the failure of the Soviet Union
to act probably lies in the calculation by Soviet leaders that
Rumania's defection was not proving very costly. It is note-
worthy that the Rumanian Government acted in a careful and
circumspect way and did not actively encourage other govern-

ments to follow its example. That is, the Rumanian Government was careful not to increase the costs of its defection to the Soviet Union, and Soviet leaders apparently concluded that the benefits of disciplinary action against Rumania did not offset its costs.

The third factor involves the probable future costs of a defection. In the Hungarian and Czechoslovak cases the situation was not stabilized but was undergoing progressive deterioration. In the Czechoslovak case, for example, Soviet and other Eastern European leaders were concerned not only with events in Czechoslovakia but with the impact of the Czechoslovak events on Eastern Europe as a whole. On May 8, 1968, East German, Polish and Bulgarian Communist leaders met with Soviet leaders in Moscow to discuss the implications of the events in Czechoslovakia, doubtless concerned with the problem of contagion or of a "demonstration effect."

The Soviet leaders probably understood that the present and future costs associated with intervention would be substantial. For example, it would make clearer the true relationship between the Soviet Union and its Eastern European clients. The hollowness of the claim of independence and the emptiness of the non-intervention pledges in the Warsaw Pact would be made evident. Intervention would also have an impact upon Communist Parties around the world, might create further cleavages in Eastern Europe, and might encourage the Western countries to pursue more active military policies in NATO. Nevertheless, from the Soviet point of view, the costs of nonintervention were increasing daily and a process of bloc disintegration may have appeared to have been under way. In the end the Soviet leaders concluded that the net benefits of intervention were greater than those of nonintervention. The rapidly rising costs of nonintervention doubtless placed a premium on action at the earliest possible moment.

Fourth, is a consideration of the available policy options and the costs and benefits associated with each. If there were political and economic control techniques available to the Soviet Union they would doubtless be considered before military intervention would be undertaken. In the cases under consideration, however, the non-military control techniques had already proved ineffective and the situation was no longer under control. Military intervention probably appeared as the means of last resort. It had one great advantage: it provided an assured means for reestablishing firm control. Under the umbrella afforded by military intervention a new set of controls could be instituted in the country in which intervention took place.

Finally, there is the impact of the passage of time on the costs and benefits associated with each policy option. Military intervention, for example, might cost more (or less) at a later date than it would at the present moment.

Because intervention is costly, neither great power will intervene in its own sphere of interest for casual reasons. Each has a threshold of toleration and will take military action only when that threshold is passed. There was some Soviet military intervention in Cuba before the missile crisis, but the United States chose not to make an issue of it. When the Russians landed missiles that readily threatened the United States, however, it did intervene. The location of a threshold is not fixed once and for all but varies with circumstances. For example, because its experience with Fidel Castro in Cuba, the United States became more concerned about the threat of Communism in Latin America. At the time of the disturbances in the Dominican Republic, therefore, the United States government acted swiftly and with overwhelming force, as if to say, "There shall be no more Castros in this hemisphere." At a time, before Castro came to power, the equivalent level of provocation might have produced nothing more than official warnings and reproaches.

Once the decision to intervene has been made, justification is not a significant problem. There is probably no intervention so outrageous that a great power will not be able, in short order, to develop a flattering justification for it. After the intervention in Czechoslovakia Soviet ideologues soon launched the doctrine of the "Socialist community." Thus *Pravda,* on September 25, 1968 published the statement that "[each Communist party] is responsible not only to its own people, but also to all the socialist countries, to the entire Communist movement. As a social system, world socialism is the common gain of the working people of all lands; it is indivisible and its defense is the common cause of all Communists and all progressives in the world, in the first place, the working folk of the socialist countries.

"Naturally the Communists of the fraternal countries could not allow the socialist states to be inactive in the name of an abstractly understood sovereignty, when they saw that the country stood in peril of antisocialist degeneration.

"There is no doubt that the actions of the five allied socialist countries in Czechoslovakia directed to the vital interests of the socialist community, and the sovereignty of socialist Czechoslovakia first and foremost, will be increasingly supported by all those who have the interest of the present revolutionary movement, of peace and security of peoples, of democracy and socialism at heart.

"People who 'disapprove' of the actions of the allied socialist states are ignoring the decisive fact that these countries are defending the interests of all, of world socialism, of the entire world revolutionary movement." [5]

The concept of a "threshold of toleration" can be spelled out in terms of a nation's cost/benefits analysis. A nation will intervene when the net benefits (i.e., benefits minus costs) of intervention are greater than the net benefits of non-intervention. It is easy to see that the location of this point will vary as the inputs into the cost-benefits analysis change.

The Monroe Doctrine offers a reasonably precise statement of the basic rule of the game for inter-bloc situations. In his Seventh Annual Message to Congress (1823) President Monroe asserted ". . . that the American continents, by the free and independent condition which they have assumed and maintain, are henceforth not to be considered as subjects for future colonization by any European powers. . . ."

The so-called "Roosevelt Corollary" to the Monroe Doctrine asserts the basic right rule of the game for intra-bloc situations, that is, the right of the predominant power to intervene in its own sphere of influence. Theodore Roosevelt, in his Annual Message in 1904, stated: "Chronic wrongdoing, or an impotence which results in a general loosening of the ties of civilized society, may in America, as elsewhere, ultimately require intervention by some civilized nation, and in the Western Hemisphere the adherence of the United States to the Monroe doctrine may force the United States, however reluctantly, in flagrant cases of such wrongdoing or impotence, to the exercise of an international police power."

Both the Soviet Union and the United States have also developed serviceable doctrines to justify covert or overt intervention in uncommitted countries. The Soviet Union intervenes in order to support "wars of liberation" against foreign or domestic oppressors. The United States finds sufficient justification for its actions in the necessity of resisting the varied threats of Communist tyranny and preserving democracy. This reasoning is the same as that used by the United States to explain hemispheric actions such as the intervention in the Dominican Republic, Guatemala and the Bay of Pigs.

DETERRENCE

Discussions of deterrence have usually centered around the possibility of nuclear attack. It is obvious however that the basic concept of deterrence can have wider application. One nation's effort to deter military action by the other need not be confined to a possible nuclear exchange but can extend to military intervention of the kinds discussed above.

While the concept of deterrence can be applied to each of the three types of great power military intervention, its utility varies with each type. In the case of inter-bloc intervention, the defending nation rarely has much of a problem in deterring attack, for the rules of the game are so clear-cut and intervention is so manifestly dangerous that no deterrent action is likely to be necessary. The basic structure of the situation provides the necessary deterrent.

Intra-bloc intervention presents quite a different deterrent problem. How is one nation to deter the other from intervening militarily in its own sphere of influence? Here also the rules of the game provide the basic framework within which attempts at deterrence must operate. These rules place an upper limit on the kind of credible threats a nation can make in trying to deter the other, since the basic rule of the game in the case of inter-bloc intervention is that the other will not deem intervention to be a *casus belli*. For example, if the United States were considering intervening militarily in Cuba it would not regard a Soviet threat of war as credible. Nor were the threats that emerged from the November, 1968, NATO meetings aimed at deterring a possible Soviet military intervention in Rumania; the NATO nations were not in a position to offer guarantees to Eastern European nations against Soviet action and therefore their threats were simply exercises in verbal militance.

There may be other ways to deter an attack. The deterring nation can make non-military threats, including threats directed toward targets other than the offending nation. The United States could scarcely threaten war in order to deter Soviet military action against an eastern Europe nation, but it might indicate that such action would hinder the achievement of Soviet-American detente, would lead to the cancellation of specific forms of collaboration, would lead to economic reprisals, and would cause the United States to take increased measures for military preparedness for other eventualities.

In addition, officials in the deterring nation should keep their minds open to the possibility of including positive inducements in its deterrent program. The objective of the defending nation is to alter the intentions of the other nation and inducements as well as threats may contribute to that end. There are many matters on which the two great powers share a common concern, and there are always actions that one *wants* the other to take (concerning trade, arms control, the United Nations, the two Germanies, China, and alliance policy, among others) as well as actions that it does *not want* the other to take.

The deterrent actions that the defending nation takes, along with any inducements it offers, will be fed into the cost/benefit calculations of the other nation. If the decision to intervene is hanging in the balance this collection of deterrents and inducements may prove decisive. On the other hand, if the threatening nation is strongly inclined to go ahead with the intervention, these deterrents and inducements will probably be insufficient to alter the balance. In many cases the deterrent program will be of marginal significance; in the case of inter-bloc intervention special deterrent actions are usually unnecessary in the case of intra-bloc intervention these actions are often unavailing.

The prospects for deterrence are more hopeful in the case of extra-bloc intervention. For one thing the stakes involved are likely to be smaller. National security will probaby not be invoved as it might be in the other two cases. The greater the potential gains from an intervention the greater the risks and costs the threatening nation will be prepared to bear. The smaller the potential gains, the smaller will be the costs and risks that it will be willing to bear and the more easily those gains can be offset by a program of deterrents. As in the case of intra-bloc intervention, the defending nation will want to consider both inducements and deterrents in trying to alter the intentions of the threatening nation; it should not confine its attention to the immediate area in contention but should range about widely. For example, if the United States were trying to deter a Soviet military intervention in the Middle East it should not focus on that area alone but should consider the deterrents and inducements open to it in connection with the United Nations, Western Europe, Eastern Europe, Southeast Asia, technical collaboration, and so on.

The deterring nation must determine: 1) what threats to make (or inducements to offer); 2) how to make those threats credible; 3) whether it will back up those threats in the event that the other nation is not deterred by them. The question of bluff is separable from the question of credibility. The first has to do with the intent of the deterring state; the second has to do with the perceptions of the intervening state. Bruce Russett has examined the factors that help establish the credibility of threats designed to deter interventions. After examining seventeen cases, he observes, ". . . the credibility of deterrence depends upon the economic, political and military interdependence of pawn and defender. Where visible ties of commerce, past or present political integration, or military cooperation exist, an attacker will be much more likely to bow before the defender's threat—or if he does not bow, he will very probably find himself at war with the defender. . . . Under these circumstances the effectiveness of the defender's threat is heavily dependent on the tangible and intangible bonds between him and the pawn. If other factors are equal, an attacker will regard a military response by the defender as more probable the greater the number of military, political, and economic ties between pawn and defender." [6]

This suggests that the deterring nation might give added credibility to threats by strengthening the bonds between itself and the third country (the pawn). For example, it can send military aid and advisors to the third nation.[7] Such actions would demonstrate its stake in the other country.

In addition, the nation trying to deter intervention must obviously be able to perform the threatened action. If the capability does not exist, the threat automatically loses all credibility. Credibility will also be increased if the nation making a threat stands to suffer substantial losses if it fails to back up its threat. The credibility of a threat is also influenced by the way in which the state considering intervention perceives the interests of the defending state. If one state says to another, "Attack us and we shall strike back with the means at our disposal," the threat will be credible, for such retaliation will be in keeping with the attacking nation's conception of the defender's interests. If one says, "Attack some other nation and we shall strike at you with all the means at our disposal," the threat is apt to be less credible. The attacker would be inclined to ask skeptically, "Do they really care that much about this other country?" If the attacker does not feel that the defending country's interests are deeply involved with the third country, it will perceive the defender's threat as disproportionate and lacking in credibility. Yet there is still room for misunderstanding. The defender might feel that, the third state is not intrinsically of vital importance, the consequences of letting the attacker's aggression go unchecked would be very serious. The way that the defending country perceives its interests is far different from the way that the attacker believes that it perceives those interests, and the stage is set for conflict.

NOTES

1. The author wishes to thank the graduate students in his seminar on international politics for their interest in discussing the ideas that appear in this paper and for their important contribution to the analysis that the paper offers.

2. See the author's *The Revolution in Statecraft: Informal Penetration* (New York, Random House, 1965), Chapter VI, and *The Functioning of the International Political System* (New York, Macmillan, 1967), Chapters 13 and 16.

3. It ought to be noted that this intervention, in such forms as economic aid, technical assistance, military assistance, is often sought by the country in which the "intervention" takes place.

4. It should be emphasized that when an observer refers to the "rules of the game" for intervention he is not signifying approval of intervention nor adopting an immoral stance. He is acting as a social scientist rather than a moralist and is seeking to analyze and understand rather than to pass judgment.

5. The full text reprinted in *The New York Times*, September 27, 1968.

6. "The Calculus of Deterence," *The Journal of Conflict Resolution* (Vol. VII, No. 2), June 1963, pp. 103, 106.

7. "In every case where the defender went to war he had previously sent military advisors and arms to the pawn." *Ibid.*

The Norms of Intervention

edited by I. William Zartman

Style or ethos in a period of international relations is a major factor in predicting the reaction and interaction of states in any specific instance. The extent to which an action can be considered a turning point depends on the degree to which it varies from the norm of the period. Czechoslovakia seems to have often been the bellwether for the "quantum" changes in international relations of this century. 1918, the end of World War I and an era in international relations, brought Czechoslovakia into being. 1938, the end of the inter-war era, saw it dismantled. 1945 brought a revival of post-war hopes and a rebirth of the republic. 1948, the advent of the Cold War, put it under Stalinist control. 1968 kept it a Soviet satellite. Only the introduction of bipolar détente in 1956 occurred without a signal from Czechoslovakia.

CZECHOSLOVAKIA, HUNGARY, POLAND, AND RUMANIA

The decisive element in the Soviet interventions of 1956 and 1968 was the degree of threat each situation posed in Soviet eyes—to the local Communist Party and its role. In

Poland in 1956, the population was practically lifeless behind the Party; there was, therefore, no problem of its losing control over internal developments. In Hungary, the situation was just the opposite: the Communist Party was disintegrating and a multiparty regime emerging. Soviet reactions differed accordingly; there was a compromise of sorts with the Polish Communist Party and military intervention in Hungary. In comparison, in Czechoslovakia during the period of democratization, various political organizations were arising which were or could become independent of the Communist Party. Still the emergence of the 231 Club and other such groups did not yet threaten the monopoly of the Communist Party, and was not as significant for the Russians as the change within the Party itself: its very rapid transformation from a Leninist-Stalinist-type of Party to the old social-democratic type that the Czechoslovak Communist Party had been at the time of its creation and well into the 1920's. If anything alarmed the Russians, it was the discovery that in Czechoslovakia they were about to deal with a socialist party and not a Communist party as they understand Communist Parties to be. One can easily conceive the Politbureau reacting the way Stalin did years earlier when he said at a Comintern congress, "The Czechoslovak Communist Party is the worst Communist Party of all, because it is the most social-democratic."

The nationalities problem had a real impact on this change. Since 1956, Slovak historians and other intellectuals had been expressing a very assertive, even nineteenth-century type of nationalism, at long last seeking the place under the sun that they had never had under the first republic or under the Communist regime. Eventually their efforts were accepted by Czech intellectuals; and other elements of the population, following the intellectuals' lead, began not only to condone Slovak aspirations but also to examine themselves and, as a result, to rediscover their own national identity. This rediscovery of Czech national identity began with the writers' congress of June 1967 and gained momentum over the following year until it attained major importance in Bohemia and Moravia; it too harked back to traditions of the nineteenth century upon which the original idea of the Czechoslovak state was based, including humanism and democratic socialism. The reassertion of national traditions of at least hundred years' standing culminated the growing desire for social change with political ramifications. Indeed, some Czechs have felt that the handling of the Slovak problem itself was one of the major reasons why the Russians reacted so violently. The Soviets were worried about liberalization generally, but they were also thinking of their own Byelorussians and Ukranians, who might find an example in the raising of the Slovaks to a level of equality with the Czechs.

In addition to the national question, economic problems also shook the orthodoxy of the Czechoslovak Communist leadership. There was an economic collapse in 1963, and Czechoslovakia had the distinction of being the only Communist country, if not the only country in the world, that suffered a decrease in its gross national product. Although a minor recovery followed, the fact remained that Czechoslovak economy was stagnating and that old formulas could not make it move again. Something had to be done, and the desire for economic reform also impelled people to think about political change. The Communist Party was vulnerable in this situation, as it had been in Hungary—if not for all the same reasons—and unlike its position in Poland in 1956.

Concerning external issues, there were also differences between the events of 1956 and 1968. The Polish claims in December 1956 were limited to domestic matters. Hungary eventually asked for Soviet acquiescence in withdrawal from the Warsaw Pact and for the recognition of a status of neutrality similar to that of Austria. Again, the Soviet reaction was very different in the two cases. This difference was carefully noted by the Czechoslovaks twelve years later, and they carefully avoided irritating issues: criticism of the Soviet Union, discussion of neutrality, reliance on the West. Thus, on the major internal and external issues, the Czechoslovak case of 1968 fell between the Poland and Hungary of 1956: "less" of a challenge to Soviet supremacy than Hungary, it nevertheless fell within the Soviet criteria for an intervention situation. Yet the comparison is not complete, for there are other contextual elements which affected the Soviet decision.

Probably the most important external element has been the West German position within the general—if diversified—Western policy of bridge-building. Of all the bridges about which the Soviets were apprehensive, those that aroused the most concern were made in Bonn. While the Soviet propaganda image of the United States and other countries has undergone changes, the Federal Republic remains a constant danger, for it remains the only country basically dissatisfied with the European status quo. The Federal Republic, which would have liked to build bridges to Moscow, where the key to unification hung, has been unable to do so because of the Democratic Republic. It therefore could build its bridges—or try to build them—only to Eastern Europe, around Pankow but not quite to Moscow. The resumption of relations with Yugoslavia was in some ways more important than the subsequent resumption of relations with Rumania, since West Germany had broken relations when Yugoslavia recognized East Germany. Thereafter were to come Czechslovakia, Hungary and Bulgaria; there was not much hope for relations with Poland, at least for the time being, which, along with the East German Republic, would then be isolated within Eastern Europe. Eventually, the hope appears to have been that Soviet influence in Eastern Europe would be reduced to manageable proportions and that the Russians would at least agree to sit down at a negotiating table with West Germany and talk about unification. Not only was the political impact of such ties with Eastern Europe a matter of apprehension for the Soviet Union, but the economic temptations that they offered also provided an alternative to Russian concepts. This possible evolution, therefore, had to be stopped.

East Germany was the one Eastern European country that had reason to feel as strongly as Russia. The threat of East German isolation by the new Western foreign policy and the threat of contagion from the liberalization program in Czechoslovakia were major factors which made it necessary for Ulbricht to step in after Bratislava and plead for intervention in Czechoslovakia. The East German considerations close the circle of analysis for they indicate that internal Czechoslovak developments were more significant in triggering the intervention than international developments. Little had changed in the nature of the German "threat" between January and August 1968. It was not necessary for Russia to take such precipitous action as armed intervention to forestall the resurgence of German power and safeguard national security. Rather, the deterioration of the Czechoslovak situation set up a condition in which the German threat might, under certain circumstances, have become a real danger. Therefore, in order of priority, internal Czechoslovak developments were paramount and the German threat secondary—even though the latter was a propaganda issue which the Russians have used with great relish. Their reaction, in sum, can be characterized as one of anticipatory apprehensiveness. The Russians were apprehensive because they anticipated future repercussions of Czechoslovak social change on their own polity, and as a result resorted to preventive aggression.

Rumania is a final element of comparison. One of the reasons why the Czechoslovak leaders had so much confidence that the Soviet Union would not intervene was that they were misled by the Rumanian example. After all, Czechoslovakia was not planning to make moves nearly as drastic as the Rumanian leaders had made, particularly in foreign policy; if Moscow exercised some restraint in not intervening in Rumania, it would take much less self-restraint not to intervene in Czechoslovakia. In fact, it was Rumania that appeared to mark a quantum change in 1968 bloc relations, were the Czechoslovak case not present to reaffirm the norm.

But there were other elements of difference which return the criteria for Soviet intervention to domestic changes rather than foreign policies. Since 1954, the Rumanian Communist Party has been the most impervious to Soviet penetration and, perhaps paradoxically, the most Stalinist. The predominant, and "ultra-orthodox," role of the Party was therefore not in question, and its cohesion served as a deterrent to intervention. Were the Russians to invade, they would be hard pressed to find a collaborationist leadership, and would have to face the prospect of running the country on their own and imposing outright military occupation. It would be too much to say that this represented a level of escalation one step above that which they would have been willing to take. But they could give Rumania a warning in Czechoslovakia, more effectively than they could give Czechoslovakia a warning in Rumania. If the prospect of quisling leadership was dim in Czechoslovakia in July and August 1968, it was still dimmer in the months to come, for if the party congresses had been held at the end of August and early September, all of the would-be collaborators would have been out of office and the Russians would have faced a united and recently, popularly approved national leadership.

In the balance, whether in 1956 or 1968, the Soviet Union intervened when it was convinced that it was about to "lose" a dominant and acceptable Communist Party regime. The reasons have always been essentially internal, even if the context is unavoidably international. The bloc cannot stand the political consequences of social change, beyond certain predictable limits. In the context of Eastern Europe, both Hungary in 1956 and Czechoslovakia in 1968 helped define these limits but were not "quantum" changes in bloc policy, whatever their impact on world politics and opinion. Only a decision *not* to intervene would have been quantum change, a subordinating internal Communist considerations in the name of "East-West good will" or respect for *inter-bloc* norms.

THE COSTS

The invasion of Czechoslovakia has been costly to the Soviet Union in ways that may not be fully understood for some time to come. The Soviets are now obliged to maintain a two-front strategy, and against a rearoused NATO. Although a serious military confrontation with China is unlikely, it has been Russian policy to maintain a military build-up on its inner Asian frontier. It is now necessary to redeploy a number of those troops outside the USSR, at some cast. That cost may be multiplied by a rub-off effect on the Russian soldiers themselves, who see themselves disliked by their fellow Communist workers and peasants and who see other ways of life (and perhaps aspirations) than in Russia.

The cost is even greater among Communist Parties outside the bloc, for the price of conformity in Eastern Europe has been dissidence in Western European Communism. The invasion of Hungary gave rise to a minority reaction of disenchantment among Western Communists, but the invasion of Czechoslovakia caused a majority wave of disaffiliation from Soviet control, notably in France, Britain, Italy, Switzerland, and Scandinavia. It would be only a slight exaggeration to say that the suppression of a "social-democratic" Communist Party in Czechoslovakia has begun to turn a number of Western European Communists into national social democrats.

The final cost is ideological. The ability of Soviet doctrine to explain present events and prescribe future courses of action has again been severely shaken, and the Russians are once more obliged to act more "Stalinistically" than they claim to think. The Brezhnev doctrine was not a refinement of ideology; it was an ex-post-facto rationalization of weakness.

AMERICAN POLICY REASONS

What considerations affected the reaction of nations outside the Soviet bloc to the invasion of Czechoslovakia? Without pretending to know the innermost thoughts of the two or at most three key decision-makers in the United States government on this matter, we can nevertheless outline the possibilities as they seemed to appear. The underlying consideration appears to have been that Czechoslovakia was not worth an atomic war to the West and that, faced with such a threat over this issue, Russia would not be the first to back down. But beyond that, there lay a deep commitment to a particular approach in East-West policy, predicted on the existence of a mutual interest in certain crucial issues. The most important of these was in hindering the use and then the spread of nuclear weapons. It was decided long ago that if the West was going to prevent proliferation, some form of collaboration with the Soviet Union was a crucial ingredient. So serious was this American commitment that Washington was prepared to sacrifice certain interests within its own alliance for the sake of this role.

The American government had also felt that some American-Soviet collaboration was essential in the Middle East, and that at some crucial moment there could be some beneficial Soviet involvement in the negotiating process on Vietnam, not simply in Paris, but generally in bringing about greater flexibility on the part of the North Vietnamese. The Government has also believed, since the first cultural agreement in 1958, that the Soviet-American cultural exchange program is to the net advantage of American long-term objectives regarding the evolution of Soviet society and policy. The United States has even been willing to accept some imbalances in its disfavor in cultural exchange for the sake of longer term, intangible objectives.

But for the very reason of their importance, every one of these particular issues was extremely difficult to use as a threat, pressure, or influence over the Soviet behavior on Czechoslovakia. The United States was unwilling to sacrifice its own interests—as it saw them—in an effort to attempt to forestall the Soviet attack. When a policy is geared to the pursuit of joint goals that a government believes to be to its net advantage and whose achievement depends on the cooperation of the other side, it becomes very difficult to lay that very policy and the underlying cooperation on the bargaining table. In such a case, the willingness to do damage to oneself for the sake of affecting the other party's intra-bloc intervention runs into strong inhibitions. In terms of gains and losses, a country hesitates to bargain away presumed greater gain for possible lesser gain.

The United States did make efforts, however, to confront the Soviets with the prospect that these matters would be seriously set back by an invasion of Czechoslovakia. Indeed, it did not take a great deal of perspicacity for the Soviets to recognize the fact without being told in so many words. But it was also said explicitly, not as a clear-cut threat, but by indicating that the political environment would be so changed by an invasion that the West might be unable to continue the non-proliferation project. However, since the warning did not have the force of a threat, it was not a credible deterrent.

Western governments have agreed that trends toward democratization or liberalization in the Soviet bloc are desirable but that the West must be extremely cautious in overtly trying to influence these trends or, indeed, in commenting on them officially. Such processes should not be turned into cold-war issues, be matters of negotiation or bargaining between the West and the Soviets, or be handled by either side as a form of intervention. For this reason, too, Western governments have refrained from appearing as the protecting powers of liberalization in Czechoslovakia or autonomy in Rumania. Indeed, in the late spring of 1968, the United States let it be known to Czechoslovakia that it could not count on American support in the case of armed intervention, a fact the Soviets too probably knew.

Most governments concluded that if there were any chance of preventing a Soviet invasion, it would depend on convincing the Soviets that, whatever the outcome in Czechoslovakia, it would not mean a forward movement of the Western frontier, militarily or politically. (Some even went so far as to argue that was the time to offer a disengagement program and a European security plan far more concrete, elaborate, and venturesome than that proposed in the joint communiqué of the NATO ministerial meeting in the spring of 1968—in fact, a Rapacki Plan—in order to give the Soviets even greater assurance that Czechoslovakia should be seen in a context of détente rather than of conflict.) In a patently delicate context, this appears to be essentially the background in which the West operated, admittedly without a great deal of hope.

COUNTERPOLICY ALTERNATIVES

Within the framework of the basic reasoning just outlined, what were the chances that the West could turn Czechoslovakia, 1968, into another type of bellwether—one marking the beginnings of a period of restraint in intrabloc interventions? The question is difficult to answer, for the search for policy alternatives operates in a narrow field of possibilities, it is hemmed in by the twin traps of the normative and the normal. The analyst tends to look at the situation as one of many of a type, from which he distills typical or normal characteristics marking the style or ethos of the period. He perceives our era as one characterized by intrabloc intervention, proclaims that the state which committed "a Dominican Republic" cannot condemn "a Czechoslovakia," and rates the two events as signs of the times, essentially inalterable givens. The critic is morally revolted by this situation. From a normative point of view, "a freedom-loving United States" cannot condone "another rape of Czechoslovakia." Yet faced with the further question whether or not the incident is worth the means of prevention and the terrible consequences which may follow, the responsible critic usually admits, with the policy-maker, that Czechoslovakia was unimportant compared with the risks of war or at least rupture with Russia.

Both the normal and the normative are often enemies of alternatives. By focussing either on what is (and therefore will be) or on what should be (but is too costly), they can obscure the search for alternative policies to acquiscence or absolute deterrence. Between the two unappealing extremes lies a field of incremental actions that can be taken by the opposing state to raise the cost of the decision to intervene or at least to probe the level of determination behind that decision. Such a search should look for means of increasing the cost of the intervention, not through a single major rise in price but through a number of small and even ambiguous raises. Rather than directly challenging the option to intervene, alternatives could be found to complicate it, circumscribe it, burden it, to impose doubts and second thoughts.

Without attempting an exhaustive listing of such alternatives, a few can be noted for consideration. One agency which could have more freely exploited was the United Nations, not as a direct but as an incremental deterrent. One of the first things the Russians asked the Czechoslovaks government to do was to withdraw their complaint from the United Nations.

They appeared to feel that this was the most important concession to extract first from the Czechs, and in fact the absence of a clear Czechoslovak voice did hamper the Western cause. It was quite clear that in the Russian calculations the possible reaction by the United Nations was high on the list. Once the matter was before the United Nations, a resolution was presented and vetoed. The United States acquiesced very quickly to the Soviet veto, although the American government could have taken the position that a veto was not possible concerning an act of aggression under Chapter VII, and that the resolution passed. The US could also have taken the matter to the General Assembly under the Uniting for Peace Resolution, as has been done in other cases. The Soviet Union has continually shown itself concerned with the legality of its actions—as the Brezhnev doctrine indicates—and with world reactions; it could have been more difficult to defend the Brezhnev doctrine in a United Nations debate than within the bloc. The very gradualness of the Czechoslovak intervention, compared with Hungary, also indicates this concern. To repeat, there is no expectation that a United Nations debate alone would have stopped the invasion. But it could have contributed to raising the cost, in conjunction with other actions.

In the beginning the Soviets insisted that their troops intervened mainly to insure the Czechoslovak border against Germany rather than to interfere domestically. The West could have warned that if Russia invaded Czechoslovakia, the bogeyman of German rearmament that the Soviets constantly cite might become real, wholly independent of American wishes. The delicacy of this argument does not invalidate it. It might also have been useful to raise technicalities of East-West relations along the Iron Curtain, such as troop ratios and military build-ups at a given distance from the border. Protests, pressures and negotiations could then bring about limitations on the extent of freedom of Soviet intervention. The United States could also have said publicly that an invasion of Czechoslovakia would lead to grave and unpredictable consequences, rather than the milder private form of warnings actually used (coupled with assurances of American intentions not to intervene). In fact, the stronger formula was later used with respect to Rumania, and reinforced more recently with respect to Austria and Yugoslavia.

Another means of indirect and incremental deterrence is through diversionary incidents, a tactic at which the Soviets are more accomplished than the West. Had the sides been reversed, a Berlin crisis would certainly have been predictable; Berlin crises always seem to appear when something else is going on! Sharply increased Western pressures on Cuba (using hijacking as an excuse) or East Germany (using Berlin as an excuse) would have served both as a warning and as a bargaining tool. Indeed, the Soviets benefitted from the very same tactic, since their intervention was "covered" by the continuing events in Vietnam and the American presidential precampaign.

Finally, even the major excuse for not rocking the international boat—the non-proliferation treaty—is open for discussion. No conclusive balance sheet has been drawn up to indicate the comparative strength of each side's desire for such a treaty, or the weight of internal divisions within the Kremlin behind and aganist the treaty. But if the Soviets can be assumed to favor such a treaty, the threat of non-ratification was a powerful one, and all the more so because the Soviets knew that the US did favor the treaty. Conversely a rapid ratification—again assuming amenable internal US processes—could have been an effective way of shifting pressure on the Soviets for ratification and at the same time strengthening pressure against intervention. Instead, the US chose an intermediate course that had no effect on the outcome either of the treaty or of the invasion.

There is no evidence that any of the alternatives mentioned above were fully discussed by the leaders of the United States government (although it would be naive to suggest that the Western response was decided on without a thorough discussion). But neither is there any evidence that any were tried (although it would be equally naive to suggest that a number of contradictory policies could be "tried" experimentally, to see what happens and then chose the best among them). What does appear is that the US acquiesced, leaving the field open to the Czechoslovak invasion, after enunciating some vague wishes and promising non-interference in the Soviet intervention. The United States gave to the USSR for Czechoslovakia the same guarantee of non-intervention that it gave seven years earlier for Cuba, despite the fact that, ideologically and geographically, the US was in a position to be to the Czechoslovak liberalization what the USSR was to the Cuban revolution. That is scarcely an example of symmetry in policy to reflect symmetry of position.

CHANGING NORMS

Like Hungary, the Czechoslovak invasion has presented the United States with both a challenge and an opportunity. The onus is now on the American government to maintain its own leadership and example, but in a way that points out the clear distinction between the methods of East and West. Russia failed before the challenge of social change among its allies. The question for the United States is whether it can do better by adapting to social change and its political consequences within the Western alliance, and still maintain its leadership role.

There are similarities between the way the United States acted in the Dominican Republic and the way the Soviets acted in Czechoslovakia. Through the Johnson doctrine, the United States indicated that it would tolerate no Communist governments in the Western Hemisphere, that it would intervene in any state that looked as if it was going to have such a government, that it reserved for itself the right to determine unilaterally whether such a government was in fact coming into existence or not, and that the US would rather be safe than sorry. Although the US was called in by—or in conjunction with—an established government, as the USSR was not, it entered under the cloak of collective self-defense organized within its regional community, talked about the style or ethos or tradition of the Western commonwealth (which in fact prohibits intervention), and coined the phrase "normalization" as the definition of the rate of change which it was prepared to bear. It would be an error to suggest that this pattern of events began in the Dominican Republic. Indeed, it would be a short range view of history to suggest that it "began" at all in the postwar world: spheres of influence have been so controlled for ages. What is striking about the Dominican Republic, is that the US followed suit.

Intervention is to be expected in the Communist bloc. Since the Communist regime was established in most of Eastern Europe through armed invasion, it is not surprising that it should be maintained in the same way. If intervention was not used against Yugoslavia, Albania, or China, there are obvious reasons. If the strict limits of Communist orthodoxy may be stretched from one period to another, the fact remains that orthodoxy is by nature limited. The theoretical and practical consequences of orthodoxy were evident well before it was given a new expression by Brezhnev.

But none of this is true with the West, where heterodoxy, pluralism, and self-determination are both theoretical tenets and practical facts. Intervention—and a fortiori preventive intervention—is an aberation, a denial of principle, and an anachronism in practice. It is obvious that the Soviet system as presently conceived cannot live with a Dubcek or a Nagy within it. It is equally obvious that the "free world system" should—by its own nature, principle, and theory—be able to live with a Bosch or even a Castro within it, particularly when it has already shown that it can stand a Batista and a Trujillo. After all Batista and Trujillo, Castro and Bosch represent the political consequence of social change—a phenomenon as desirable as it is inevitable. It may be argued that intervention does not seek to stop social change but merely to keep the political consequences from going "too far." Even in theory such reasoning is dubious, and in practice, the end is unlikely to be attained from the outside. The United States recognized this very limitation on effectiveness when it opposed the Suez intervention. The Communist system can only deal with the political consequences of social change through intervention. The West has no such limitation on its abilities and hence no justification for such intervention. If intervention becomes characteristic of world relations, not just of the East, and if spheres of influence harden to the point where invasion is practiced and condoned by both sides, a quantum change in the world will indeed have taken place, but one that marks the freezing of social change—and in fact, human freedom. It is for the West to show that we are not there yet and by the same token to shape a norm of ethos of the times that inhibits intervention within an alliance as well as outside.

Index